LEGA
MATURITY

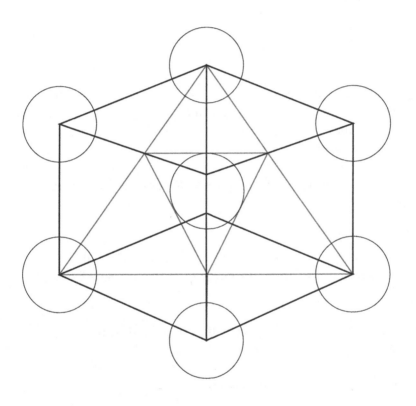

Ricky Nieuwenhuis
and
Lindi Masters

Contents

Chapter 1

We Can All See

It is imperative in these days that we start seeing the unfolding of *our* the testimony scroll which sits inside each of us. *NO ~~this~~ scroll in heaven. We scroll = bk of life.*

As I've been travelling to various conferences over the past few years, people have been coming to me with the same desperate question, "Rick, how do you see? I want to see the way you see." My response has been, "How do I see?"

They don't know how to answer because in their belief system and thought process, they have formulated an idea of how I see even though I've never spoken about how I see. I speak about what I see.

During conferences I would share an encounter that I had experienced and condense it into a story so it could become a framework for the listeners to engage with. My testimony would become a gateway for those hearing it, giving them an opportunity to trade with it through finances or the desire of their heart so it could become their portion, because that's what testimony is. It means to be duplicated. This made me look at my own journey and how I've activated my spiritual eyes to behold. I have realized it is important for those we are walking with to speak about how we see and to bring it back down to the core foundation. My heart's desire is for people to have a framework to engage with as I help to facilitate their ability to see.

his testimony become theirs? NO

Whose core foundation

There are two key issues that have closed peoples' gateways and their ability to see:

" any more than few

behold, focus on

A) Religion *[handwritten: ?]*
B) Confession *[handwritten: ?]*

A. RELIGION

Paul says in **2 Corinthians 3:14**, "But their minds were blinded. For until this day the same veil remains unlifted in the reading of the Old Testament, because the veil is taken away in Christ."

[handwritten: sin, iniquity, idolatry]

That veil is the spirit of religion which has become so entrenched into the Church that we have traded into it, adopted that way of thinking, and applied it to our lives. This has closed the gate for us to see and to engage within the Kingdom realms and has created a doctrine that says not every person can see. That doctrine is not scriptural. *[handwritten: Religion has closed gate? Which]*

[handwritten: Religions other religious idolatry]

In the process of maturing, we have to untangle ourselves from religious belief systems that we have traded into which speak other than the truth that Yahweh speaks to us when we engage by the Spirit.

In **John 3:3** we read, "Jesus answered and said to him, 'Most assuredly, I say to you, unless one is born again, he cannot see the kingdom of God.'"

[handwritten: salvation = save heal deliver]

If we are born again we have the capacity to see. The truth of salvation is that it's not just a religious prayer to be saved. Salvation is an encounter to engage with Yeshua who is the New and Living Way. *[handwritten: No it may or may not be an encounter]*

It is stated in **Hebrews 10:19-20**, "Therefore, brethren, having boldness to enter the Holiest by the blood of Jesus, by a new and living way which He consecrated for us, through the veil, that is, His flesh."

Salvation cleansed ~~by~~ of sin   when we believe in
by blood of Christ   No Jesus only way truly
we

This gives us the ability and capacity to step into Him so that we *are*
can begin to unlock the fulness that is our portion. If we reduce *already*
salvation to our level of understanding - which is connected to *there*
the religious spirit, structure, and system - then the foundation of *Nt*
our salvation is going to be a man-made prayer, that still works *Jesus*
because of Yahweh's grace, but does not give us the capacity to
see. That is something we must be fully aware of when we engage.
We must disentangle ourselves from religious belief systems,
concepts, and ideas. *SIN, iniquity, tresspasses*

B. CONFESSION *(CURSING self)*

The second thing that hinders us from seeing is the doctrine based
on our inability to see because of the veil that covers our heart.
This allows us to confess that we cannot see, thereby framing the
government we carry into creation, entering the new day through
the frequency spoken the day before. As a result, we cannot see.

We read in **Proverbs 18:21**, "Death and life are in the power of the *7*
tongue, and those who love it will eat its fruit."

No God activates this   Not all are
Within ourselves we need to deal with the fact that we can see! *seers*
Every person in Christ (who has said 'yes' to this journey) is a new *prophets*
creation seated with Yeshua in heavenly places. We can activate *think*
our spiritual man, giving us the capacity to behold all things *he aware*
that are in the Kingdom. This is the reality but we have to renew *to*
our mind which works against the spiritual encounters that are *will not love*
unfolding if we have traded into the religious system that is under
the sun. There is a conflict going on between who we are as sons,
seated in heavenly places, and the unrenewed mind which wars *unbelief*
against that truth that Yahweh has revealed to us. If we do not
continuously engage with the truth we will fall back to the default
setting of trading into the religious structure, believing we cannot

No engage in Father son Hs

9

The Lord then it's chooses to open our eyes
we do not have of
any framework

see.

Activating our spiritual eye to see requires work and effort to
build a framework and foundation to allow His Kingdom to be
revealed in us. It requires that we untangle ourselves from religion
and instead behold the mysteries that Yeshua wants to reveal by
engaging and repenting. This word, repent, does not mean to say
sorry, which is under the sun (this is the system of the world, and
man's morality, corrupted at the fall of Lucifer.) Repentance is
going in to behold the countenance of all that is unfolding in the
Kingdom realms, because what we behold is what we will become.
If we just say sorry under the sun, it will only be a matter of time
before we have to repent and apologise again for doing the same
thing. Saying sorry is a process that keeps us in bondage instead of
going in to behold and to engage. Seeing what is unfolding for us
as sons within This Day is what transforms us.

repentance is turning 180 degrees

As sons, seated in the midst of creation, seeing is a huge part of
who we are. A key component of governing is seeing. When we
hear the word 'see' we take all the knowledge we have of it under
the sun and apply it to our mystical life. We then fall short of our
expectations and are disappointed which results in us having to
navigate a journey because of the failure of an expectation we had
which was under the sun. *eyes to see both natural*
+ spiritual Gov is His given authority

We must understand what seeing is. When we begin to behold as
a son, we must wipe away any preconceived ideas or concepts that
we have regarding seeing under the sun. It must be deleted from
our memory because that process will not work. If we engage the
things that are under the sun and connected to the natural world
and use them to connect to the supernatural, they will always fall
short of what Yahweh has positioned for us within the realm of
truth. When we engage, we must firstly understand the way we
are fashioned and formed. When we begin to arc with who we are,

10

we see an alignment taking place which opens gateways for us.
We are then able to engage, to see, to govern, and to administrate
from our position of government so that things not only shift
within our lives but also within creation. *see discernment, Revelation*

We are a three-part being of body, soul, and spirit. In the Church
Age we were taught that we see through a gift called prophecy.
This is an amazing gift and within the mystic community we have
seen moments where sons have prophesied – not from under
the sun – and have brought about massive transformation. The
gift of prophecy under the sun has linked itself to the religious
structure of the Church and has become one of the stumbling
blocks within the mystic community because of the law of first
mention of how we see. When we see something happening in a
person's life, whether negatively or positively, we will use the gift
of prophecy and say, "Brother, I see this about you." We then begin
to speak from the place of gifting, under the sun, into that person
regarding what we have seen. If we are in a corporate setting and
operating in the gift of prophecy it will let others, who do not have
this gift, think that they cannot see because they don't prophesy.
They will begin to think that they need the gift of prophecy to see.
wrong teaching – all don't prophesy

As I've walked through this process I've seen how Yahweh *reality*
has revealed truth in me and I've had to see it for what it is.
Sometimes we try to justify the very things that have become a
veil in our lives that has blinded us from seeing. The system has
taught us how to see by masquerading itself as truth which has
been inferior truth. We have been taught to see from the external,
processing it through the gateways of our eyes to allow it to be
situated within us, but the way Yeshua taught how one sees is from
the inside out. The ability to see and behold should come through
the gate of Yeshua. When He was seated in the seat of creation, He
modelled what it looks like to be a Son seated in heavenly places
within creation. He lived, moved, and had His being within the

ALL transformation is from the inside out

Kingdom but also here in creation. He saw from the inside of who He was, outwards.

If someone says they cannot see, they have admitted to themselves that the twenty gates within them, seated in the three-part being of who they are, are inactive. These twenty gates which give us the ability to see, are situated within our body, soul, and spirit. Because of the Church Age teachings, doctrines and mind-sets, people believe they can only see through one gate, which are the eyes within the body. All the others are waiting for us to engage with them and activate them so we can behold and frame things. We must engage with the encounter of salvation and not the prayer of salvation.

A. SPIRIT

Our spirit-man, which is seated within our body, has eight gates:

where in Bibles

Prayer
Reverence (deep respect for Yahweh)
Faith
Hope
Worship
Revelation
Intuition
Fear of God

By spending time engaging and pursuing, these eight gates give us the ability to behold and lead us into our soul which also has gates in it.

prayer ? ? NO

There is not a lot of prayer on the face of the earth. Religious prayers shift nothing! Prayer is engaging through tongues, which is praying in the spirit, and is connected to our spirit. This gate opens into the next gate and the next until it opens into the soul realm.

[handwritten annotation: God Father, Son, HS living TRANSFORMATION]

Engaging through faith and hope also open gateways.

Worship brings about transformation. It is not about singing a few songs on a Sunday that are about us, our problems and waiting to be filled because we came to Church empty. Worship is not just singing songs but a way of life that demonstrates to creation our intimacy and union with Yahweh and all that is found within the Kingdom that comes through every gateway of who we are. The religious system and structure has taught us that singing to Yahweh is worship but this has become a ceiling because the religious spirit knows that if we know this truth, transformation will come into creation.

Revelation is something that is revealed to us that doesn't just come through teachings. It's about being seated and positioned within the Kingdom realms and whatever we are engaging with is transforming us and we become that revelation to creation. Revelation is not a 'light-bulb moment' but us becoming the revelation, which is a gateway, which opens up to our soul.

[handwritten annotation: NO revelation exists from teaching the... ; No Not whatever — JC, HS]

Intuition is the ability to understand something instinctively without the need for conscious reasoning. We don't need to be persuaded because we are transformed whilst seated in the Kingdom realms, and within the instinct of who we are we know that what we are walking out is true within our function and position within creation.

The fear of God is reverent fear, giving us the ability to govern with Yahweh. It is not the fear that we speak about when under the sun within the religious system and structure.

[handwritten annotation: Fear of God faith obedience]

[handwritten annotation: Satan ~~under earth~~ is @ 2nd heaven, earth]

If we take that structure we will never behold the countenance of

13

Yahweh because fear is entrenched in us.

The majority of us as believers must repent for the way we have viewed our soul. We feel our soul is the biggest issue in who we are on the earth and our ability to be a son seated in heavenly places and the dishonour that we've shown towards our soul needs to be rectified. We need to trade out some of the things we have spoken, to behold the position of sonship that we carry.

B. SOUL

Within the soul we have the following seven gates:

Conscience (moral sense of right and wrong)
Reason
Imagination   *unsanctified*
Mind
Emotion
Choice   *will is choice*
Will

When I started to honour the gate of imagination, it opened up for me to begin to behold the Kingdom.

C. BODY

We have five gates in the body:

Sight   *Body   Soul*
Hearing   *natural world*
Touch
Smell
Taste

Once we honour the process of our body, those five gates open and because of the flow happening from within, it flows into

14

creation. That is when we become the transition point from the Kingdom realms within us being evident in creation flowing out and making a massive impact to the area we rule, reign, and govern from.

We must honour our gate and begin to engage with the being of who we are so that the flow comes from deep within us and from the Kingdom realms that are sitting within us. The Kingdom realms are not 'out there somewhere' that come through the miraculous, they are in us. When we begin to sit in that place of union with Yahweh and all that is within the Kingdom starts *Spirit* flowing through the chambers of who we are, we begin to access *NO* our spirit-man and then the eight gates are activated and open up to flow into our soul realm and we begin to see and behold what is happening within the soul, which activate and open up the seven gates which in turn flow through and activate the five gates of the body as we honour our body here in creation. The moment we begin to open the gateway of our eyes or the gateway of feeling it now begins to flow as streams of living water, impacting creation. All of this starts with the realization of what is happening on the inside of us.

When we begin to honour this process we realize there is no longer any dishonour to any parts of our being because the moment one is dishonoured it brings everything out of alignment and then we cannot see. We have to honour each gate to bring an alignment so that when it activates it builds a framework for us to begin to see.

Spirit   8 gates
Soul   7 gates
Body   5 gates
Total   20 gates

When we bring these twenty gates down to their lowest mathematical form it equals two. In Hebrew, *Beyt* means house and this letter has a gematria of two. We have always been designed to be a house. We are the house, the tabernacle, and the dwelling place of the God-head, who have gates waiting to see the transformation that is happening within us as we are seated within creation so that we can begin to release and reveal all the things we are becoming there, here.

In **Matthew 6:10** we read, "Your kingdom come. Your will be done, on earth as it is in heaven."

Within the Church Age we prayed that prayer but didn't have the revelation of where heaven is going to come from. We are all still waiting for it to one day come through the galaxies, stars, and planets, through a miracle, because we've set the atmosphere beautifully through worship. We might get glimpses of gold dust and begin to look at the sign forgetting that the sign is pointing to who we are and through Whom all these things come from.

The majority of the way I see, is through feeling. I honour that gate which is connected to the other four gates of who I am in my body. These are connected to the seven gates of my soul which are connected to the eight gates of my spirit-man that is connected to the function of the government that I carry as I am seated with Him in heavenly places in Christ. Because of my position within Yeshua everything begins to align and build a framework through which I go in to behold and to see. This all came about from honouring the gate of feeling.

People will say that they felt something but they want to see. They, in fact, just saw but because they didn't honour the gateway of feeling, dishonour was released which brings everything out of calibration and they only begin to feel things physically because of

16

being positioned once again under the sun.

When I am seated within the place of government, my access point is through faith. My spirit-man is connected to Faith and Hope who are Beings as well as laws. The Being of Faith came and engaged with me and when I honoured the feeling, all the other gates aligned and built a framework and when I began to behold him everything started to unfold because of my honouring. Faith becomes the gate for us to engage and see things seated in heavenly places.

Hebrews 11:1, "Now faith is the substance of things hoped for, the evidence of things not seen."

The other gate within our spirit-man is hope. Faith and Hope arc together to allow us the ability to behold spiritually. As I honoured Faith and Hope as they arced together, they gave me the ability to behold through this framework where Yahweh shared some mysteries of His Kingdom with me. When I started to honour this, the pathway which was Faith allowed me to go in and be seated there to behold, through my imagination, what Yahweh was unfolding. If we govern our body correctly then our imagination should be a gate that is going to edify all things coming from the Kingdom. If we don't govern our body correctly or are watching things we shouldn't be watching or feeling things we shouldn't be feeling, and those gates are corrupted, our imagination is going to be corrupted. We can then ask ourselves the question, "Am I seeing the way I'm supposed to be seeing?" If we are governing correctly, our imagination is going to sanctify all things that we engage with.

When I go through the process and the twenty gates are arcing together, they build a framework. Faith is a huge part of my engagement in the Kingdom and I have an incredible relationship with the Beings of Faith and Hope, but within this process of maturity and walking it out my initial gateway to these realms, is faith. When we step into Faith and we begin to walk with Faith we create a pathway which gives us access so we don't have to go through the strategic protocol of going into the Kingdom through Faith, but can now start walking on that path because of the maturity we carry as a son.

When my wife and I first bought our property I received keys and I had to go through the whole bunch to find the access key. Once I located it I was able to gain access through the gate and before I knew it, that access point was so easy to step in and walk through without being consciously aware of what I was doing.

During the process of going through the gates mentioned, we walk in and become the protocol and can enter into our seat of government because we don't rely on external protocol. We should be able to go in, to engage. Within this process of maturity we must get to the place where we become the protocol, and our union with the Being of Faith and all the other gates are so aligned that we can go in, in a moment, without having to spend time preparing an atmosphere through prayer, meditation and worship. I'm a son. I've learned about the gates, they've unfolded, I've gone in and now as I step into that place as a son, I spend time with my Father and engage with Him even though I'm still seated here, because of the alignment.

We do not have the right to say to ourselves that we cannot see! Seeing comes through desire and belief. Belief is a realm. When a father came to Yeshua and was asking for help for his son, he asked Yeshua to help his unbelief. He knew that what Yeshua was saying was true and he knew that there was a realm for him and his family which was their portion, but he needed help with his unbelief because he knew belief was a realm that could open up healing. The moment he said that, Yeshua healed his son because that realm opened for the father and he saw the fruit multiply within the area of government that he carried.

This is recorded in **Mark 9:24**, "Immediately the father of the child cried out and said with tears, "Lord, I believe; help my unbelief!""

For me, as a son, seated with my Father in Christ in heavenly places, honouring my body, soul, and spirit, honouring where I am positioned and governing from, those gates open up and I begin to see it established and I see the fruit manifest.

Chapter 2
Ability To See

So many people have asked the question, "How do I get to see?" Ian talks about seeing, and specifically about the division of soul and spirit. Many have been working hard at this issue, wanting to see our soul and spirit divided but finding it difficult. We were actually born with the division but have lost our joy in the process of trying to become these spirit beings, people who can see. If we've lost our joy, we've lost everything because the joy of the Lord is our strength. If we've lost our strength, we've lost everything in the ability to see and to do what Yahweh wants us to do. I was born seeing. Every one of us were born seeing.

Psalm 91:5 says, "You shall not be afraid of the terror by night, nor of the arrow that flies by day."

This Scripture speaks about the terror by night. The children's movie, Monster's, Inc. is a real story because these demonic beings come through a gate or door and into our house or into our room and frighten us at night. The sole purpose of the terror by night is to shut our ability to see, both the bad and the good. Throughout my childhood I was terrified of what I could see. My oldest child didn't have night terrors. My second child was five years old and woke me up several times during the night saying he was scared. My youngest would also say he was afraid at night. When my middle child was older, we were in England together and I was talking about the terror by night. He remembered what he experienced as a child and how things would crawl down the wall from the air vents. As a result, he shut his ability to see. I told him I was sorry that I had scolded him for waking me up to which he responded, "Wait, I could always see!"

We must be careful to not shut down the good with the bad, because anything outside of the physical 'normal' we put into the same category of the 'scary things' and we don't want to be around it. We must remember that we can see! Why would our sight open up its doors if we dishonour the ability to see? Honour is a door, so when we say we can see, that whole realm turns and moves towards us. The doors of sight, imagination and seeing into the realms of the Kingdom are right next to us and when we say we cannot see, it all shuts down and turns away until we're ready to turn and look at it.

Sometimes we don't know how we actually 'see' in the Kingdom. A while ago I saw something and I was asked if I saw it with my physical eyes or with my spirit. I answered that I didn't know because for me, the two have become one, but I honour both. When I honour both, they turn towards me and present themselves and then I start to see them as physical matter.

— prior to holographic understanding ?

Ezekiel saw holographic images that became solid objects when he saw the chariot in Chapter one and Chapter ten because he viewed them through Yahweh's created light. He was seeing waves of frequency and when he turned his attention to it and looked at it through created light, the waves started to change through observation. Quantum physics talks about observation being really important by observing waves that become matter. Faith is the substance of things hoped for and the evidence of things not yet seen. When we look at the door with intent and start hoping for it and giving our attention to it, we start seeing the waves and frequency of the door. It starts to become physical matter which we can actually feel.

Once I was on a long-haul flight, where I started to engage, and

21

stepped out of the plane in the spirit. I saw a dais under my feet and I started to push against the clouds and the turbulence. I did this all by faith, seeing what the turbulence looked like in the cloud formations. Thereafter, whenever I flew, I would push the clouds and turbulence away, and it went from 'by faith' to actual physical matter. I pushed and I could literally feel the turbulence as I was pushing it away. I had practiced this by faith many times before I actually physically felt it. Every time I had stepped into this realm I found a dais under my feet.

At never he came brattles — seeing in by spirit

Ezekiel was seeing a spiritual encounter which became matter because he measured it through created light and framed it into existence. This sums up that faith is the substance of things hoped for. Observation is important because when we observe it through created light it takes on matter. If we don't observe it through created light it will never take on matter. Much of our sight has stuttered and stumbled because we don't observe, so instead, we shrug it off saying it was our imagination, so it doesn't take traction because we don't observe it. Ian Clayton doesn't have to go through the processes others have to go through to see, to feel, to touch because he's been doing it for many years. He might not necessarily turn to something to look at it, but I do because I'm very tactile and I need to see and feel, so I turn to look. Whenever I see spiritual energy around a person (I might see a flash of light), I look at it and before I speak I turn my intent and observation towards it and look at it and speak to it saying, "Angel, I know you're there." The door opens because it knows I want to engage and the angel takes on form and I see what it looks like. The door opens wider and I can start seeing the other angels and other things around them. I never discount the experience. I have given it form and matter by observation. This is how I've taught myself to continually see.

A number of years ago, because of my background and what my

22

family were dabbling in, I always saw the demonic realm. It was normal for me to see demons and the strong man and it was a frightening time of going up mountains and being blown off them and encountering crazy weather. It was also an exciting time and I loved casting out demons. They were scared of me because of Yeshua in me. It was incredibly easy for me to see into that realm because I was born seeing. I asked Yahweh to open my eyes to the angelic realm. I had come from the old Church Age structure that said we were not allowed to talk to angels except for the three that are mentioned in the Word and it was all fear based. I was a bit nervous to look into that realm. Up to that point I *needs* had seen Yeshua physically and some of the angelic, but ninety- *Deliuer* nine percent of my everyday was demonic. It was wonderful to *ance* begin to turn and I had to re-teach myself how to see because it was natural for me to see the demonic realm. Now I had to teach myself to engage so I could see the angelic realm and push the demonic aside. When I did that, I realized that they stopped manifesting around me. *I No Father Sou Hs demons took form of angels - beautiful acts of ouil good*

Many years ago, Ian taught on familiar spirits, saying how we *good* create our own demons. Familiar spirits are attached to us because *No - focus* of the access given to them generationally through cellular *open doors* memory. When we get born again, **2 Corinthians 5:17** says, "Therefore, if anyone is in Christ, he is a new creation; old things have passed away; behold, all things have become new."

When I became born from above, I woke up the next morning and my body was the same as the day before. My spirit was the same because it's given to us by Yahweh, so what changed? It was my soul, but in the Church Age and in deliverance we're taught that it's our soul that needs to be dealt with. We're taught there's *both* no good thing in the flesh and we're always beating up the soul *sin & God* but Scripture says all things have become new. My old soul was gone, so why was my new soul manifesting the things that I had to deal with before I got saved?

I realized that it was generational cellular memory whispering in my ear, bringing to remembrance issues I had with rejection, which I had grown up with. I saw back as far as 1802 in my written family line. As soon as I turned my attention towards the frequency of rejection and looked at it through created light, it took on physical form and rejection became a demon in me which I had to cast out of myself. *No Hs/God deLiocRs*

Unhekl mi super natral God

The best thing I've ever done is learn how to go into my DNA strand, take out what looked like dark balls or spots, go to the Throne of Grace, wash them in the blood of the Lamb, repent for allowing the frequency of rejection to be embedded in my DNA and when it was beautifully transformed I put it back into my DNA strand and I started to redeem and set myself free.

me I ular in Jesus

I did deliverance with someone and cast out the demon which was not big at all, just a skull looking at us. When we looked at it I remarked how small it was and how much trouble it had given her. She said she couldn't believe it but while she was looking at it, a spirit of fear came over her and she said, "But I'm still so frightened of it." The minute she said that it grew from a skull to a six-foot demon in front of us. She had just grown her own demon! How did she do that? She had turned to a familiar spirit and given her attention to it. *focus*

Often, within the whole issue of sight, we are still giving attention to and looking into the realm of the familiars. We have to be careful with a familiar spirit that we've accessed before, and that has been bothering us, because it affects our sight. A lot of us do not see properly because we're stuck within an Old Age. We know we've entered a New Age and everything has changed and is new but we can still be stuck within the old way of doing things by applying new terminologies:

Jesus is the same yesterday to day o to morrow

24

- The old way of seeing in the prophetic
- The old way of being an intercessor
- Applying these old ways into the new

We've heard statements saying that the five-fold ministry is finished. It's not finished as in no longer here, but it is finished in its current form because Yahweh is about to raise it up into the form that it should have been in. At the moment the prophetic movement is in carnage and Yahweh is saying He will fix this.

There is an old model available to us to show us how to see. It shows us what's coming and what the future is going to be. It's a narrative and tells us about the mark of the beast and how we're going to be persecuted. When we turn prophetically we turn into that narrative, look at it and give life to it and we begin to speak it. In this case, the prophetic has not moved away from the old but is still looking through the door of the familiar spirit, and preaching the same stuff.

I used to do what we called 'popcorn prophecy'. There would be two or three hundred people in a room and we would prophesy over everyone! Yeshua never did that but I felt sorry for the people who had come waiting for a word. After a while I would feel the prophetic lift off me so I would go into worship and sing in tongues until I felt myself enter into something. I was tapping into their familiars without knowing it and these familiars were telling me that the person had a hard life and that certain things happened to them. I would hear this and I would speak to the person who would look at me saying, "How did you know that?" Then I would say, "The Lord says …." and I'd give them an encouragement.

This in itself was not wrong, but was I pressing into the future, the

25

olam, the everlasting, bringing something that was calling those
things that be not as though they were? This is done by quantum
physics, taking their frequency out of their scroll, and landing it
right in front of them. My flesh wanted to bless everybody but
I was trading on the familiars and I repented for this. The old
prophetic movement had a way of seeing and I travelled as a
prophet for three years. I've had to train myself out of it, saying to
Yahweh that I would not prophesy unless I saw clearly what was
coming from the olam. Since I've done that, when I get the words,
I have an encounter either seeing something very dramatically or
I have a dream encounter. It will be framed up and it will show me
what's coming and I will be able to say, "Thus says the Lord God
Almighty, this is coming." Or I take what I see in the future and
pull it into the present. *that is what the prophets is. see clearly no mix tone*

The trading of the old way has stopped us from seeing in the new
way and we need to ask the Lord to help us see. Our desire to see
is the compass of our house and our heart. Scripture says in **Psalm
37:4**, "Delight yourself also in the Lord, and He shall give you the
desires of your heart." Yahweh gives us the compass and honours
that. We need to activate our heart and activate our desire. It is a
dishonour to the Holy Spirit who sits inside of us to continuously
say we cannot see. *Ruach haKodesh* breathes inside of us to give
us the ability to see but because of the dishonour, He shuts down.
NO describe dream w/God 'NO desires within soul, boi.

Most of us have peripheral vision, where we see things out of the
corners of our eyes. We might have chosen to not look at what we
saw because of fear, but that was our sight. We should with intent,
turn to it and observe the frequency or the wave and walk towards
it. Then looking within we ask what we see. If it is demonic, we
can deal with it, but if it's not we can engage. *Discernment*

Interpretation from Bible

Once, Ian and I were having lunch with a group of people. As we
were chatting amongst ourselves I saw a flash of light behind Ian. I

turned to it and gave it my attention. This is the whole issue about our compass, activating the house of desire because we want to see it. When I did that, I saw this Being standing behind Ian and it wasn't his angel. Then Ian turned to look behind him, looked up and down at what he saw and carried on eating. He saw me grinning at him and he just nodded his head and concentrated on his meal.

How did this happen? It came through desire. I saw it and he felt it, acknowledged it, framed it up and carried on. The compass on the inside of us must be activated through honour so we can begin to see. Yahweh is calling us to maturity. He is about to do something spectacular on the face of the earth.

I actuale self

No God miracle.

Some years ago I had a foster child living with me. He's a Zulu boy and there were a lot of ancestral spirits hanging around him. When he was about ten years old there was a time when he would growl at me every time he walked past me! I would look at him and he'd be acting like a normal boy, but there was something in him that didn't like me at all. I began to lay hands on him while he was sleeping, anoint him with oil and told these entities to leave him. One night he sat bolt upright, looked me in the eye and said, "I'm sick of this." I asked, "Sick of what?" "Everything!" it growled, then he went back to sleep like a normal ten-year-old.

I knew I had to get rid of what was calling him on the inside. A few days later he lost control and started destroying my kitchen and my dining room. My daughter came to see what was going on and over his head I told her, "We have to do this now." I never wanted to cast demons out of a ten-year-old and this was an unusual and specific event. She was holding him down and he was biting her while we were casting the demons out. We were on the kitchen floor wrestling this child and when he was finished, he stood up and he said he could see. He could see clearly. He said, "Mommy, I'm too scared to sleep in my room because I'm scared of those dark men in my room. I want to sleep in your room because I like those light men."

I took my seventeen-year-old with me and told him we would get rid of the dark men in his room. We went into the room and I saw them standing in the four corners. I told my son to cast them out of the room. He looked at me and said, "Mom, I can't see them!" I could have said to him, "It's all right, I'll do it." No, as a mom this is where we go, "Stop it! Open your eyes and see them!" He blinked and said, "I see them." He then cast them out the room. That's how I taught my seventeen-year-old to see.

We must believe what we see instead of enabling ourselves to not see. I believed what I saw and I believed that my son saw too, and I believed that the ten-year-old was seeing. This comes from activating the desire. At no point in my entire existence have I ever said that I cannot see. But what I have done, at a detriment to me, was ask God to stop all the dreams I was having. I had small children at the time and because of not sleeping properly at night, I was really tired. When I did that, I stopped dreaming for seven years.

When we say we can't see or we don't want to see, there is a process of seven years where we possibly won't see or dream. I know a psalmist who did this. He shut it down for seven years because he dishonoured the door until it started to slowly open up again. If we've dishonoured the gifting, we can go to the Mobile Court to get it re-opened.

I've asked Marios Ellinas to teach the Hubs how to engage with Honour. This is one of the pivotal stages of the next phase and era we've stepped into during this pandemic time. When we come out of this, we're stepping into a New Era. We cannot be immature because this will prevent us from going in. It's time to deal with our issues and stop hiding behind our hurts. Everybody has been hurt by the Church. If we deal with our issues and just get on with our lives, these things will not bother us. *Right* *r*

Maturity requires that we honour every encounter that we have had and we work through it and into it so Yahweh can show us what it is that He want to do with us. We're living in an 'instant' society where we want instant access to everything. We have encounters and then call for the next one. That is not the point of an encounter. We must re-visit them and not waste them. Once the gate has opened and we've honoured the house of desire and walked through it, the gate will always be open to us and for us, to show others how to go in. Maturity requires that we don't waste these encounters. *No the gate closes if we move into sin, iniquity, transgression*

We read in **Matthew 25:23**, "His lord said to him, 'Well done, good and faithful servant; you have been faithful over a few things, I will make you ruler over many things. Enter into the joy of your lord.'"

Coming into this place of seeing and having more encounters gets you into a place of joy, into the joy of the Lord, the joy of the Master. It's a joyful experience! If you lose your joy in your encounters and your seeing, you will lose everything. Some people are logical and require certain steps to be put into place which will open up the door so they can step in. This process still requires faith. It has to be done by faith. It can't be touched, it's not tangible. Faith is mystical but also a Being, so when we turn and engage and love on Faith, Faith turns towards us and begins to bring the law of faith to arc with us and once the two of them arc they roll out a carpet of favour and the Being of Favour starts to show us things. We have to know Faith and we have to engage.

Because of the intent of our heart, our compass, and our desire, it begins to show us in a physical manifestation that which we are wanting. We must not waste our encounters or our sight by looking for the next thing. Let's enjoy the journey. We must be faithful in the few things so we can become ruler of much. This pathway begins to open up many realms to us and matures us as sons.

ACTIVATION

Shut your eyes and imagine your front door. Describe the door to yourself, down to the smallest detail. Go through your door and enter your house. Look around. What does it look like? In your imagination describe your house to yourself.

My point here is that you aren't at the door and yet you can describe it. Your ability to use your imaginative door is alive and well. Now by faith you will step through the veil of His flesh. I did this many times by faith until one day I entered and actually felt what was like a membrane on my face and I pushed through to the other side.

Father, we thank You for Your grace and mercy as we go to the Mobile Court.

As we are in the Mobile Court today Father, we ask You that if there is any wicked way in us, if we've done anything that was wrong this week which does not come from Your throne, we ask You to forgive us and set us free. We repent and thank You that we can walk in freedom.

Now we're going to pray for someone we know who might need healing or comfort and we're going to let them know.

Close your eyes and step through the veil of His flesh, which is the new and living way, by which we enter into the Throne of Grace. When we step through the veil by faith, we arc with our natural body and go that room or place by faith. This is the body that looks like us. We're not there, we are here but it looks like us. Many times people have seen my natural body but I'm not even in that country.

Take your natural body and stand in front of that person and pray for them and lay your hands on them to release whatever it is that they need. When you do that, be aware of what they're wearing, where they are, their surroundings. This is part of learning how to see. You must learn to trust what you see.

Now, step through the veil of His flesh into the realms of His Kingdom. We can now step in boldly to the throne of grace.
Breathe in His name. By faith see Him standing in front of you.
Breathe in His frequency, hold it and breathe it out.
Breathe in the frequency of heaven and hold it.
Breathe out - Yod Hey Vav Hey.
Breathe in.
Breathe out - Yod Hey Vav Hey.
We activate the *Aleph* sitting in our upper chest area, the breath.

We now take our natural body, which is part of our six bodies, and we're going to go to that person by thought speed and look at them. Don't say you can't see them! You know them, so imagine them. If you're struggling with this, look at a photograph of them. As you are looking at them, pray for them.

If they need healing, lay hands on them, and say, "Father I release healing to them." Our hands are gates which release the Kingdom of Yahweh and healing into their body.

If you are praying for comfort or finances, pray it over them and release it over them. Yod Hey Vav Hey.

31

Look at what they're wearing and begin to see around the room. Your fragrance and your frequency are also in that room and they know you're there.

Release it from within you over them – healing, money, jobs etcetera. Pray over them and touch their body from the top of their heads to the soles of their feet; from the *Keter* to the *Malkhut*. We release the fragrance of Yeshua into the room and leave our peace and blessing in that whole room. Let it touch everybody that is there.

Now we're going to come back out of there.

I encourage you to phone them and ask them if they saw you or tell them what you saw. They might tell you that they weren't wearing that or weren't in the place you describe. That's alright because you are learning to turn your intent to a door and opening it so it can engage with you. Because you're honouring the encounter and the door, you're activating the house of desire. If you didn't get it right, just tell them you'll try again because you need to keep activating sight and the ability to go in and to do things.

Intercession is turning into the current situation and playing catch up with what has happened instead of bringing the future into the present so we are not caught unawares. We must not say we're going to have to pray harder! We know how to pray, why must it be harder? This is old school Christian talk. We want to reach into the future and bring it into the present.

There are the upper waters and the lower waters – the upper *Mem* and the lower *Mem* – which mirror one another. When your lower *Mem* is in chaos it means your upper *Mem* has not come through the *Tifferet* (through our belly) and dealt with the issues in order to bring peace and balance to what is going on, including in our countries. When our country is a mess, it's because the lower waters are reflecting the upper waters and we, the *ecclesia*, are a mess! We get the government we deserve because it reflects what we are doing. If we were operating as true, mature sons, the government would have to begin to reflect what is happening in the heavens above.

I want us to run on the walls of our cities.

I used to take a map and put it out for my oracles. We have kings, priests, legislators, and oracles. We're a king, we look after the people; we're a priest, we take it up and down before the Father; we're legislators and legislate what we see; but the oracle sees into the *olam* and takes what they see and bring it into the present. This is a mature son, a god-man. This is the one new man.

I would kneel on the map and look at the circumference of each country seeing through the gateway of imagination tall walls rise up on the boundaries of every country and then I would step on that wall. From being in the natural, I would suddenly have physical matter and I saw the Prince Warring Angel. I asked him if I had permission to run on the walls with him and to arc with him. He gave me permission. I then saw all the other warring angels on the walls and other angels too, running on the walls of the countries and looking in. I began to run on the walls with the angels. I didn't pray anything, and I didn't say, "God get rid of that President." Instead I said, "Father, I pray that You send out Your warring angels to come and to bring peace to this land and to show mercy to this land."

This brings me to **Joel 2:9a**, "They run to and fro in the city, They run on the wall." Together, let us stand on the maps of our nations and run on the walls.

A lady I knew told me that Yahweh told her we must pray for

Estonia. I looked at the map and saw it was a tiny country which used to be part of Russia but got its independence.
I took Estonia and put it in my heart and every time I thought of Estonia, I would say, "Estonia, I love you."

What I'm doing with my sight is seeing the country of Estonia in my heart and I'm feeling her because she sits in me. We began to run on the walls, and as we did this we asked the Prince Warring Angel to send out the warring angels to protect the borders from invasion again, only to discover that there was talk of another invasion, and so within three months of engaging in this way, Britain had all of a sudden sent 800 troops to the border of Estonia to protect them.

I want you to run on the walls of your country. I want you to see it again in the realms of the Kingdom. See the circumference of your country and see the walls come up. By faith I want you to engage it and let it become matter. Stand on the wall and I want you to see the Prince Warring Angel.

Prince Warring Angel, we honour you and we want to thank you that we are on our country's walls. We honour you and ask if we can come together and arc with you for our Nation's sake?

Now, begin to run on the walls, around and around, arcing together with the angelic hosts. Father, we ask that You send on that country (name your country), warring angels to go out and do what they have to do to bring the country to obedience, fruitfulness, and peace. We release it on our Nations.
There are many issues in every Nation and we're not going to name them all but you can ask the angels to release it. You don't have to do it they will do it. We send out the warring angels on our behalf to bring peace to the land.

See warring angels being sent out right now, watch them running out and taking the sword of the Spirit and taking scrolls and begin to speak to the right people to change what's going on in your nation. Warfare got a whole lot easier and more interesting than it used to be! Father, we release the angels and undertake to run on the walls.

I'm activating your sight and your ability to see. Run on your Nation, feel the walls and release the angelic. I want you to do this by faith, creating it and creating matter. See yourself on the walls and the angels going out, arcing with Faith and the Law of Faith so that Favour engages and rolls out like a carpet in front of you. We bless our Nations by running on the walls, by standing together and bringing peace like Joel's army.

Your country is calling out for mature sons, not babies and people panicking and being reactionary all the time. We're bringing in peace and good policy and bringing in what Yahweh wants to do.

Yod Hey Vav Hey.

We release finances in our Nation. We release peace and the right people in government. Yahweh puts people in and removes people. We thank You for the angelic which expose evil and shout it from the roof tops, exposing corruption. We stand with the angelic hosts on the walls of our Nation and we govern as mature sons. This is where the whole of creation turns and looks at you and begins to manifest. It is waiting for you. Not only is the earth waiting for you but your own flesh is waiting for you. I've just seen a flash in the studio, and as I turned and began to speak about creation, this angelic Being manifested right in front of me because I turned my attention to it and honoured it. That honour opened a door because my heart's desire opened up through honour.

35

Creation has never shouted as loud as it's shouting during this time. Sons, it's time to mature and govern. We mustn't be distracted by this pandemic because there is some sort of outbreak every one-hundred years. We will survive this one but we must govern and not let ourselves be distracted but rather turn our attention into Yahweh, becoming one mind and bringing upon the face of the earth that which He wants us to bring by activating our sight and our ability to see. Not grabbing onto old familiars and old ways of seeing but determining to turn our attention to the door of hope and desire and through intent, creating matter out of frequency.

Chapter 3
Unfolding Your Mountain

When we engage we start seeing the function and then we see the fruit. We honour every little thing which is massive in the greater scheme of things. The word 'mountain' has been used a lot but we don't necessarily have the full framework for what it actually is. My mountain has completely shifted my perspective in terms of the government that I carry both in the Kingdom realm and the natural realm. My testimony will be able to be your portion as you honour it and go in by faith so that you can begin to see it manifest within your life.

We sit and govern from within our mountains. Our physical body is the tabernacle and dwelling place for the fullness of Yahweh's Kingdom to be positioned and as we are strategically placed within creation we are able to administrate things and see things shift.

When we did the activation of running on the walls of our cities, we were operating from our mountain. By faith we activated our mountain by stepping into it and from that place of government we started to run. That is the function of our mountain.

Our mountain and our government are connected to us as we are positioned within creation. The first mention of 'house' in Scripture (which is us) is found in **Genesis 28** and tells the story of Jacob's encounter. I've had encounters with Jacob which have started to transform some things within me and my personal life. **Genesis 28:17** says, "And he was afraid and said, 'How awesome is this place! This is none other than the house of God, and this is the gate of heaven!'" Prior to this, Jacob laid his head upon a stone to rest during the night. When he had that encounter Yahweh began to speak the mysteries and the secrets of His Kingdom to Jacob and when he came out of the encounter he said, "This is the house of God, the gate of heaven." House means dwelling place or tabernacle or ark and the gate means a transition point. We've spoken about the twenty gates that are seated within us as we are strategically seated within creation.

As we honour the house of God, which is us, and honour what is happening spiritually, our mountain is waiting for us in the Kingdom realm which we are able to access by salvation which comes through an encounter with Yeshua. As a son, seated there, we see things unfolding for us because of our desire and yearning and we can begin to explore our mountain which sits above us, arcing with who we are, as a son seated in creation, unfolding the mystery of what is happening there and echoing it here. It's all about government.

There are important protocols that we must understand and step into so we can begin to behold a mystery, to get a grid and a framework for it to begin to step in and see it unfold. The more aware we are of what's happening the more the transformation takes place within us and establishing the Kingdom realms to who we are as we walk out the testimony scroll that Yahweh has for us and what creation is waiting to unfold within us.

Many of my personal encounters have come from **Romans 8**. When we behold truth and see it for what it is, something happens within us that we can't contain. Scripture says this in **Romans 8:12-13**, "Therefore, brethren, we are debtors—not to the flesh, to live according to the flesh. For if you live according to the flesh you will die; but if by the Spirit you put to death the deeds of the body, you will live." This is talking about maturity and dealing with things inside of us.

Romans 8:14-19, "For as many as are led by the Spirit of God, these are sons of God. For you did not receive the spirit of bondage again to fear, but you received the Spirit of adoption by whom we cry out, 'Abba, Father.' The Spirit Himself bears witness with our spirit that we are children of God, and if children, then heirs—heirs of God and joint heirs with Christ, if indeed we suffer with Him, that we may also be glorified together. For I consider that the sufferings of this present time are not worthy to be compared with the glory which shall be revealed in us. For the earnest expectation of the creation eagerly waits for the revealing of the sons of God." When creation is mentioned here, we mustn't think about what is just created under the sun. Creation is everything that has been created. Creation is waiting for us, in our rightful position, to be revealed as sons.

Romans 8:20-21, "For the creation was subjected to futility, not willingly, but because of Him who subjected it in hope; because the creation itself also will be delivered from the bondage of corruption into the glorious liberty of the children of God." We have been taught, under the sun, that hope is wishful thinking. This hope that Paul is talking about is the joyful anticipation of the goodness of what Yahweh is about to unfold within our day, which comes through us and our gates. This is what creation has seen.

Because of what Yeshua did at Calvary, He became the gateway for us. He is our transition point, our Saviour into the Kingdom realms. Who is creation's saviour? It's us! This Scripture doesn't say that creation will be brought into the freedom of the glory of the rapture. It also doesn't say that creation will be brought into the freedom of the glory of Yeshua when He returns. Scripture says that creation will be taken from bondage to decay and be brought into the glorious freedom and liberty *of the children of God*. This is the reason we speak at length about maturity. If we get this right, everything else will come into its glorious freedom and liberty because of who we are becoming. I am so passionate about this because I was entrenched within the system. The system is putting the authority and the mandate which should be upon us on Yeshua and Yahweh, where we wait for them to do something, yet Scripture says that creation is waiting for us!

I was doing an Origin Gate Podcast (www.origingate.com) a few months ago, speaking from **Romans 8**. When I finished, I locked up the office and walked out and when I turned, I saw my whole back yard. Light was emanating out from the being of who I am, and as far as I could see within the light, creation was in its First Estate. I'm still trying to figure out exactly what I saw but I can tell you that this portion of Scripture was arcing with the encounter that unfolded through the twenty different gateways and I realised I was glancing into a hope that creation had seen and was communicating to me because it is in me. We've been taught that creation is external and we're positioned in creation with everything around us. Scripture says everything is within Yahweh, and in **John 17:21** Yeshua said to the Father, "That they all may be one, as You, Father, are in Me, and I in You; that they also may be one in Us, that the world may believe that You sent Me." This is complete union. While I was looking out at creation, creation was within me and it realized that I was aware of what was happening. I was arcing with the hope and they said, "Rick, what you have seen is what you are becoming." They had seen the hope which is joyful anticipation of what is about to unfold.

We go after this because we are so desperate to see the unfolding mystery take place for us as sons, and as we put value on what is happening, it will change not only us but everything we sit over. As we are being transformed through this process of maturity and things are shifting within us, when we walk in creation, even though creation is within us, we walk with this understanding that as we govern from our mountain, which is seated above us. We begin to rule, reign and govern from that place, arcing with our physical body here that has many elements, we then realize that creation is looking at the revealing of what we are becoming, sons in maturity; taking responsibility, doing the work, governing, going in and beholding transformation taking place so that it transforms us here. We know what is happening spiritually, even if it's by faith, and a glimpse opens up and creation shows us what it has seen because it's looking at a son who is growing up into maturity, taking creation from bondage to decay and bringing it into the glorious freedom and liberty of who we are becoming. It's a massive responsibility.

The Church Age and the religious spirit, which backs the religious system, tries to devalue the truth in who we are here as a son. Within the Church Age, we don't like to take responsibility; we blame everyone else including God, but there's a shift happening and we realize that Scripture says in **Psalm 115:16** that, "The heaven, even the heavens, are the Lord's; but the earth He has given to the children of men." If we are seated here and seated there, we get to rule and reign with our Father.

When I started to understand that there is a mountain that is mine that I can go into, I was so excited and wanted to know what my mountain looked like. By faith I went through this process of going through the gate of my imagination. Prior to that I was sitting over my life, governing it and making sure that all my gates were in alignment, so that when the imagination gate opened up I knew it was going to enhance my portion. As I sat in my gate I started to see my mountain unfold. By faith I started to see its structure as it became clearer and then realized that the mountain was sitting above me and at the same time sitting within me and arcing with creation. I even saw the angels ascending and descending as I was seated on my mountain as they were coming back to release who they are in me and the mandate that's on my life within creation. One of the angels seemed different to the other angels and he was sitting on my mountain, on the seat of authority.

The Kingdom of Heaven is a serious place but the Beings also love to surprise and to be surprised when they see us engaging with this process. As I went up my mountain I knew I had to take the seat of authority because when we sit on our mountain everything changes. My angel was watching me and I started to arc with him and introduced myself and he spoke back to me. We are taught in the Church Age to not talk to angels but so many men and women in Scripture engaged and talked to angels. When Peter arrived at the house where the believers were praying, they thought that his angel was there, but it was him. As I engaged with my angel, who was sitting on my mountain, he stood up and shifted to the side, walked past me and turned around. A moment took place where a son, seated in maturity, who had gone through the process of engaging, had gone up his mountain and sat on it. When I sat on my mountain, everything within my mountain and everything within creation that I sit, rule and reign over, turned and looked at me. The honour and the respect that came from everything that looked up to me was so incredible because they saw me in my seat of authority which was positioned within Yeshua. Because I was in Him, it gave me the authority to step into my function and position so when creation saw me it was as if I was the Father, seated on my mountain to rule, reign and govern. That is responsibility.

In **Psalm 8:4-5** Scripture says, "What is man that You are mindful of him, and the son of man that You visit him? For You have made him a little lower than the angels, and You have crowned him with glory and honour."

As things shift, it's about what I declare and say to every area that I sit over which brings about a transformation instead of sitting in a prayer meeting asking God to move on my behalf. This prayer comes from Christians who are not in maturity and who have traded into the religious system and spirit which has caused them to believe that there's a void between them and Yahweh. They are trusting in the giftings and hoping they are sufficient enough for transformation. If they indeed worked we would be governing from the Kingdom these past two thousand years and not be dealing with what we're dealing with at the moment.

There is a maturity rising up on the face of the earth where we are in a place of government, understanding our function, and seated in our mountain where we begin to look over areas so we can rule, reign, and govern by releasing what we are becoming over that area. As I was exploring these realms I didn't just want the answers to my questions, I wanted to become the answer without me saying a word so I could manifest what I had become. We want answers so we can speak about it for people to hear. I care about my function as a son and the transformation happening within me and what creation has seen within me. From bondage to decay, brought into what I am becoming as a son.

I was sitting over a particular area in a seat of government that opened up for my neighbourhood. This will first start with our own house, which is our body, because if we can't govern our own body then we can forget about the nation. We must make sure that we're seated on our own mountain, having gone through the process, our gates opening up so that we can go by faith into these areas. The assignment will be positioned upon us so we can begin to release that which we see. During my night watch I went over my area and I was holding it within my heart, because my suburb, city and nation are in me even though I'm in them because of where we are seated in Christ. I saw a particular area and thought to myself that this was not right. I was still growing in maturity and I felt a holy anger and thought that this had to change. There are things we say and do where Yahweh will just correct us. As I looked at this problem area, I started to judge it and Yahweh spoke to me and said, "Son, the very area that you just brought judgement upon is the true reflection of the lack of your sonship over that area."

Yahweh was teaching me that it's not about bringing judgment but about bringing a transformation because of what we have become! When we look at that area and see it's out of alignment and not reflecting the truth of what the Kingdom wants, we go up to become it in the transformation – however long it takes – we sit in that place, and when we come back down as a son and look over it, that area will look up to us and then it has hope. What is the hope? Creation can become what that son has become.

We must get rid of the old mind-set and thought process of religion where we're taught to speak over an area 'in the Name of Jesus.' The seven sons of Sceva did it and look what happened to them when they started commanding demons without being positioned in Yeshua. We must be positioned as a son in our governing.

I engaged with my angel who sits over my mountain. His name is Breaker. He carries a sledgehammer with him that arcs together with me, within my position as a son within government, and when I walk with an assignment from Yahweh he begins to walk in a co-labouring relationship with me and he begins to do things as I do things and we arc together. If we are in the place of engaging, seated within our mountain, and we haven't asked who our angel is or where he is seated, he will be on top of our mountain above the seat. We must arc with our angel and communicate with him by introducing ourselves and he will speak with us.

When I started to understand what was unfolding within my mountain spiritually that was arcing with my temple, the dwelling place where I am, I came across a Scripture that was always read in a particular way when I was in the Church Age during a prayer meeting. **Isaiah 54:2** reads, "Enlarge the place of your tent, and let them stretch out the curtains of your dwellings; do not spare; lengthen your cords, and strengthen your stakes." There is a difference between the Church Age mind-set where we pray for God to extend our tent pegs and fill our meeting place, and the mind-set of sons seated within the heavenly realms. It's not about Yahweh doing anything, it's about us doing it. It says *we* need to enlarge *our* tents and *we* need to stretch out the curtains of *our* dwelling place. When we walk within this process of maturity and begin to go in and engage with our mountain spiritually, there's an arcing taking place. Because of our level of maturity and our responsibility, Yahweh can trust us to extend our tent pegs.

When I started to engage with this, I understood my physical body, I understood my temple. I then began to understand that I have a spiritual mountain. When I went in and came back out, what would transform me there would transform me here. It got to a place of me carrying the responsibility for this particular area where Yahweh would communicate with me through a co-labouring union and relationship and I realized I could extend my tent peg and begin to expand over a region because of my maturity and the fruit I have seen. When I expanded, my mountain expanded and the government that sits upon me expanded. I walked this process out from my body, my household, my neighbourhood, my city, my nation. There are things that have happened within my nation because of the journey of responsibility and the government that I've carried. Our responsibility is to sit over our mountain, to extend the tent pegs, so that we can begin to rule, reign, and govern over creation as we co-labour with Yahweh.

A few years ago South Africa had the worst drought ever recorded. There was no rain at all and while I was engaging I was watching the news. They were speaking about the drought and we were experiencing water cuts. Two weeks later I was in my office engaging with Yahweh and I was taken back to the time I heard the news clip reporting that we were in a severe drought. The South African government was starting to make deals with other nations to bring in water. Suddenly I experienced a holy anger. I closed my eyes and instantly found myself in my mountain in the spiritual realm and looking over the clouds and the ocean. I was in my extended place within the government of my mountain. For the first time, my mountain arced with Yahweh's Mountain which is perfect. My mountain is within His Mountain and His is within mine and all our mountains are positioned within us. Yahweh started to speak to me and to teach me about governing. He said, "Look out at those clouds. Creation is waiting for the revealing of a son." I realized the mandate, I realized the responsibility and I knew that the next action that I took was either going to keep us in a drought by tapping out of the assignment because of religious belief systems telling me who I'm not, or I could trade into the Mountain of Yahweh that started to reveal to me the assignment and the responsibility that I carry as a son. The choice was mine.

I said, "Yahweh, I'm ready." I looked out over the clouds, which is creation, and they were waiting for a revealing of a son in maturity that is seated within his government in his mountain. An authority came upon me and I shouted out, "Come forth!" The clouds, which are living substance, turned to the voice, and started coming towards me. I was seated within my mountain within my government of authority arcing with Yahweh's Mountain and the clouds were coming to the voice that called them. Then I heard a bang and found myself back in my office. There was thunder and lightning outside making the windows of my office vibrate. As I was processing what had just happened, I heard drops of rain on my office roof. I stepped outside and looked up to where I had seen the clouds, and they were the same clouds I had seen within my mountain, in the place of government operating within a place of maturity, coming over my property. They started to roll over our nation and it rained for four days.

A moment of doubt came in my mind so I checked the weather app on my phone and it said no rain for the next few weeks and yet it was pouring! This was the fruit of a son positioned in his mountain, operating from the place of government, arcing with Yahweh's Mountain and things began to move. Every strategically placed dam within the nation was filled. Four days later the same news desk that ran the story on the drought two weeks prior ran an article which they called The Four-Day Miracle. They could not understand how something could shift within a matter of minutes from a weather forecast that had no rain in sight, to a downpour of such magnitude. Creation was moving from bondage to decay into the glorious freedom of the children of God and we see the effects taking place. Our nations are a living substance with boundaries and corner stones, not just land, and they are waiting for us to sit over their walls and run upon them while we're seated in our mountain and arcing with Yahweh's Mountain. Things happen as we begin to release and reveal who we are becoming.

This temple, the body that we sit in, is faultless because of our position within Yeshua which immediately qualifies us for the assignment that Yahweh has given us. It's living a surrendered life, the truth of salvation, entering into Christ – the new and living way – to step in to behold all things that are our portion. Our spiritual mountain, where we arc with our angel and where we are seated in government, is flawless and arcs together with Yahweh's

Mountain which is perfect. There is importance with a faultless, flawless, perfect mountain arcing together as a three-strand cord to reveal an establishment of what we are becoming in creation and which it has seen and which it is becoming.

What if we get to the place of taking responsibility for our lives, our mountain, going in and engaging with Yahweh, being transformed and transfigured within this process? Every teaching we hear that produces revelation leads us into an encounter so we can arc with the teaching on the other side. If we don't do that we'll become more religious in nature because these teachings produce knowledge. If knowledge does not lead us into an encounter we're going to be doing things religiously and expecting results.

One day we're going to not see a deterioration in anything because of the government that we are going to carry, including life. Paul says that the glory resting on us is ever increasing. We can shift the deterioration of creation that is in bondage right now to bring it into the glorious freedom and liberty so that when we extend our tent pegs, because of our position within the seat of authority within the government that we carry, creation can go from glory to glory as we have been transformed from glory to glory. Is it possible that we can enter into a day where death no longer becomes the gateway for people to enter into the spiritual realm?

My heart's desire is that generations to come won't have to plan for their retirement, which will give them a certain amount of time on the earth before they die, because we're going to change and cultivate mindsets within people and we will see the fruit of never dying. What does that look like? I have no idea but I'm going after it! If I don't frame it, generations to come won't walk in their inheritance of what we're trading into. When we trade and put value on something that has touched our heart, something happens. My wife and I trade as Yahweh prompts us and it has become a lifestyle that is glorious because we cannot outgive God. If we don't trade, we will always live with our finances under the sun.

Chapter 4
Engaging Your Mountain

True sonship is people rising up as the one new man. It doesn't look like a Greek or Jew but looks like one who is totally covered, totally engrossed with and encompassed by Yeshua so we look like Him, we smell like Him, we act like Him. There's no differentiation but completely putting on Christ, putting on the mind of Christ and becoming that one new man.

When I first saw my mountains I was engaging in the garden of my heart and when I went into my garden for the first time, I looked in the distance and I saw seven mountains. I went with this Being to the mountains and saw that I had a sword in my hand. A dragon was sitting on the mountain and I was able to slay it with my sword so I could sit on my seat. That began the process of me understanding my mountains and engaging with them.

God will facilitate His glory from two places:
From Jerusalem, with the twelve laws of Jerusalem, and from Zion, with the twelve laws of Zion. The book of Zechariah tells us about Joshua, the high priest, who went into the Court with filthy garments which were taken off.

Zechariah 3:7 talks about these laws, "Thus says the Lord of hosts: 'If you will walk in My ways, and if you will keep My command, then you shall also judge My house, and likewise have charge of My courts; I will give you places to walk among these who stand here.'"
The word for 'ways' is 'laws' in the original, which are the twelve laws of Jerusalem and Zion which are in the Mountain of Yahweh.

Ephesians 2:5-7, "Even when we were dead in trespasses, made us alive together with Christ (by grace you have been saved), and raised us up together, and made us sit together in the heavenly places in Christ Jesus, that in the ages to come He might show the exceeding riches of His grace in His kindness toward us in Christ Jesus."

The word 'places' is not in the original manuscript, so it would read in the heavenlies and in the realms. Our functionality in God is empowering us to become rulers, to sit as those who are mature sons, kings and priests, legislators, and oracles ruling and reigning in Yahweh.

The parable of the talents teaches us about coming into a place of rulership. Out of rulership comes rest and out of rest comes rulership. Bob Jones said this is a decade of rest, that Yahweh has been looking for a people who are in rest so that He can find His dwelling place in them. This is not laziness or taking a holiday, because you can have a busy rest or an unproductive rest. Rest is a place of resting, even when all hell breaks loose, and we find our shalom. We centre ourselves in Him and that's our place of rest.

The Mountain of God is a place of rulership and it's also the house of God and the throne room of God where the throne sits on top of the Mountain of Yahweh. In **Psalm 24:3-4a** we read, "Who may ascend into the hill of the Lord? Or who may stand in His holy place? He who has clean hands and a pure heart." Scripture uses the word *into* not *onto*, so we know a mountain isn't just a pretty place with trees and grass growing on it but it is a place of government. Whenever we see the word 'mountain', as in who can ascend into the mountain or into the hill of the Lord, that's where Yahweh is sitting on His throne. He who has clean hands and a pure heart, which is the intent of his heart, is able to go into that mountain to govern with Him, seated with Him in that mountain.

In **Matthew 14:23** Scripture says, "And when He had sent the multitudes away, He went up on the mountain by Himself to pray. Now when evening came, He was alone there." When He went into that realm of government and was face to face with Yahweh, He said He would only do what the Father told Him to do. When He came back from that place He was on the mountain and He saw the disciples on the water. There's a good chance He wasn't near the water to see the disciples, which means that in the realm of the government of the mountain that He was in, by the Spirit He saw where the disciples were. It wasn't necessarily about Him sitting on a physical mountain and Him seeing the disciples way down on the water.

The Seat of Rest Within Me

This is something we all struggle with because rest is a huge issue. Rest is not something that the 21st century embraces or walks in. We've just done a podcast for Wisdom's Echo and in it I speak that we have this resting where we go on holiday and come back saying we're exhausted and need a rest from our holiday. These are things called 'busy rest' and that's not rest. What is rest? How do we find this place of rest? Where is the seat of rest? Sometimes we can sit back and watch TV and still not be in rest because our mind is active and thinking about all the things that need to be done.
We have six bodies.
Our natural body that looks like us and is seen in different places.
Our physical, carnal body which is the body that we live in.
Our spiritual body.
Our terrestrial body.
Our celestial body.
Our god-body.

Everything we do operates from the cube within us. We are the cube and the cube sits within us. These five bodies culminate in the god-body when all our bodies are operating together, understanding each other, seeing each other, and connecting to each other all the time. The god-body is the enochian body that Enoch had when he had all his bodies synergising and arcing together and he fully manifested the god-body. The spiritual body is the one talked about in **Ephesians 2:6** which says, "And raised us up together, and made us sit together in the heavenly places in Christ Jesus." This seat becomes our seat of government and rest seated on top of our mountain. The God-head of Father, Son and Spirit are there as well as us in our spirit, soul, and body and we begin to synergize together as we look at the God-head in divine union and sovereignty. This is how we become one who walks in divine sovereignty and union with Yahweh. We are seated with Christ in heavenly places in our seat of rest sitting inside of us. Where is that placed?

Here is an example: my *physical carnal body* is on earth, lying in bed sleeping. My spirit and my soul start engaging with my *spiritual body*, the one seated with Christ in heavenly places, where I enter in through the veil of His flesh because His blood gives me access so I can sit on the seat of rest. My *natural body* can also be traversing on the earth and my terrestrial body goes to and fro on the face of the earth. My *celestial body* is engaging above the stars and the sun and the moon. This is not under the sun, but engaging in celestial matters. This is the law of quantum entanglement, where we separate two photons and when one moves, the other moves simultaneously. My body, which is lying on the bed starts to arc with this spiritual body and quantum entanglement takes place.

Often, when we feel something on the inside is not quite right, we're quantumly entangling with our spiritual body which has turned to see something and our natural or carnal body does the same thing. To use an old Church Age saying we would say, "I feel uneasy," which would then make us speak in tongues and go into warfare mode. Our terrestrial body doesn't look like our natural or carnal body even though it is us. It's in a spiritual form going to and fro on the face of the earth. If it sees an earthquake coming, the carnal body feels that something is not right. In old school speak we would say, "I feel the Holy Spirit saying there's an earthquake coming." What if it's our terrestrial body turning and looking and our physical carnal body is turning and looking at the same time because we are arcing together?

Ruach haKodesh begins to let me know, when I'm running on the face of the earth in my terrestrial body, that there's an imminent earthquake, so my carnal body picks up that one is coming and I can pray and engage. This is how I engage with my different bodies. Something might be happening celestially and my celestial body will turn to the celestial council (not everybody goes there). I might feel that something is happening in the stars, something going on in the realm of the atmosphere, that I've got to look into and engage with and pray in tongues. What's happening is that there's an arcing together of my two bodies.

My seat of rest is on the inside of me, within my belly. We have on the inside of us something that I would call the cube. Where does it place me when I look at this cube? I know I'm seated with Christ in heavenly places and I'm going to and fro on the face of the earth. I'm a celestial, natural and carnal body and my god-body is operating from within, so I can place all these bodies on a cube within me. It is not an external but an internal thing.

Without Yeshua we have to engage all the protocols of the law to engage with the cube. Within Yeshua, because of the blood of the Lamb, this becomes internal and sits on the inside of us so we activate the six bodies within us which are also external because of quantum entanglement. The whole cube sits within us and flows out of us and that's how we operate from within. The seat of rest is within us and out of our belly flow rivers of living water.

True government and operating in rulership come from within. I love some of the ancient books like the *Sefer Yetzirah* because of how they engage with the mysteries and what they teach. However, because of the blood of Yeshua, my access is now instantaneous because of Him and I no longer have need of these protocols. We rule and reign from within.

The Kingdom is within me but it is also external on the inside of Him. I am made a little lower than Elohim, I'm a fully-fledged son, with all of this operating. That's why He was able to say to the Sadducees and the Pharisees in **John 10:34**, "Jesus answered them, 'Is it not written in your law, "I said, 'You are gods?'"' They were angry because He called Himself a god. Yeshua was a Rabbi and understood the law and Scriptures which say, 'You are gods.' If anyone preached this in Christendom, they were persecuted.

The only way I can be a god, made a little lower than Elohim, is by having the cube functioning within me; the god-bodies all functioning within me, understanding my throne, my seat of rest. When I get born from above, Yeshua and the *Ruach haKodesh* overshadow me and help me to learn how to function on my governmental seat of rest. As I mature and grow up in Yahweh and I learn how to deal with my issues and my DNA and all these things, I then begin to take over and am able to rule and reign as a son and Yeshua allows me to because Father, Son and Holy Spirit and my body, soul and spirit are arcing together all the time. As I look and engage with Yahweh from a distance by looking at Him, seeing Him, and smelling Him, I move towards looking at Him face-to-face. I see what He sees, I smell what He smells and I taste what He tastes. I hear what He says because I'm so close and I breathe Him in.

When I step through the veil of His flesh and breathe Him in He's not far, He's right here, as close as my hand is to my mouth. Everything sits within the Mountain of Yahweh and He sits on the throne. The seat of rest is within me and establishes the government of God within me.

I had to deal with the dragon on my mountain and kill it and then sit on my mountain. I also have my ministry mountain, both local and internationally, my business and work mountains, my art and authoring books mountain, my family mountain, and there are certain governmental things I'm allowed to sit on. I have a seventh mountain which I haven't engaged with yet and these are things that I saw when I went into the garden of my heart.

FIRST ACTIVATION

We will now engage with the garden of our heart and try and see our mountain. We begin to engage by taking our physical, carnal body through the veil of His flesh, stepping in to Yeshua.

Yod, Hey, Vav, Hey.

When we're in Him we live and move and have our being. Now we're going to step into the river of God taking this whole body and the cube within, into the realms of His Kingdom. I want you to feel yourself standing in the river of God that flows from His throne. Look at your feet and at the water running right through you. There could be scrolls, fish, pebbles, gold, precious stones or whatever you see, and you can pick them up and take them into your garden or put them in your mountain.

Walk up the river to the waterfall and then go up the waterfall in thought speed. At the top you will step off onto land where there will be a gate in front of you. It could be an archway, a wooden gate, covered over or whatever it is, I want you to clean it up and open it up. By faith I want you to step through that gateway and into the enclosed garden of your heart.

This is the place of encounter and fellowship with Yeshua. You don't take problems in there or other people in there, it's not a place of fellowship for the rest of your people, it's for you and Yeshua to engage in intimacy and sweetness. Look around, there might be things you have to fix and clean-up which will be for another time. There should be a place for you to sit where Yeshua will communicate with you.

I want you to lift up your eyes and in the distance I want you to see your mountains. I want you to learn how to go to those mountains. They all have names which will come to you which will be things like your business mountain, your family mountain, your personal mountain, your ministry mountain. Whatever those mountains are, Yahweh will show you what they are as you begin to sit on your seat or throne on top of each mountain. If there is a dragon there, it's only there because you've not taken ownership and rulership, so for those of you in business today, I'm telling you to go on to your business mountain and make sure you clean up all the junk that's sitting on there because you haven't engaged that mountain, so that you can sit on that seat and can begin to govern your business from a seat of rulership. Take up the Sword of the Spirit and slice up the dragon.

I've learned that with dragons you cut off the head, you cut off their arms and legs and then cut off their tail. If you don't cut off their tail then in old Christian language you will get 'back-lash'. I also slit open the belly. Every time I've done this, different things have fallen out. I once received a children's book on dragons which someone found in a charity store in London that the Dragonology Society in our area had published in the 1600s. Everything mentioned had a dragon; there was a dragon of water, a dragon of the forest, a dragon for different things. In this children's story they would have to go to the dragon and inside its belly there would be a scroll in a little pocket and the children would write a letter telling the dragon how much they loved it and would stick the letter in the pocket.

They understood that a dragon steals your inheritance and it steals your scroll so every time I saw a dragon I would cut off its head, legs, and tail. The reason I know it causes backlash is because once I didn't cut off its tail and ended up having a claw stuck in my skull and my eye for two weeks. I no longer do deliverance because I know how to go into the Courts, but I asked someone to pray with me. She told me she saw a dragon claw stuck in my head so I knew I had backlash because I hadn't dealt with it properly. You can go to the Mobile Courts if you have to, if it's a big dragon, and get your papers because it's an accusation against you. Once you have the papers it can't touch you.

I took over a Church in England and when I slit open the stomach of a dragon I found sitting on their mountain, out of its belly fell several scalps. Normally we would take the treasure that falls out of the belly of the dragon because it's for us to put into our mountain or to trade on the Sea of Glass for the future generations of this particular mountain. I asked Yahweh what this was and He told me these were the scalps of the people that the dragon had eaten and spat out but that I would stop it. I took the scalps and traded them into the Sea of Glass, spoke life over those who had planted the work before I got there and within two days I met one of the founders of the group.

They had terrible things happen. People had become sick, people had divorced, people got cancer and I was able to bring restoration and peace to the mountain because Yahweh had said that I was the one who would stop this from happening and there would be no more death to this particular work.

Before Rick started dating Melanie, Yahweh told us that he would be our Timothy. They got married, my husband transitioned to glory and within four years I knew that I was going to move to England as I had been given the call by Yahweh to move there. We were able to transition Rick and Mel into the work, as he was always ear-marked to run the work here, so I went to England to start something there. The Breaker angel that Ricky has was the angel that I had walked with, and when I left for England, I left without him. When I got to England I looked around asking myself where the angel was and then remembered that I had left the angel behind for Rick as an inheritance. Ian often says that you pack up a mountain and unpack it but I had left a mountain behind and went out and started a new mountain so Rick didn't have to start out afresh. You never give your children nothing to start with, you give them a foundation to bounce off of.

I was in the realms of the Kingdom and I saw this mountain of Shiloh (the Church) and I saw a dragon, wearing a red cape, wrapped around this mountain. I could see a scroll in its belly that had diamonds and precious stones and finances embedded in it. I remember saying to myself, "This is Rick and Mel's job." I was moving around the mountain calling, "Ricky and Mel, the mountain needs to be redeemed!" I phoned Mel the next day asking her where she was as I had been calling to her. I told her about the mountain and the dragon and that they had to deal into it. A time later, Ricky saw the dragon with the red cape and killed it and opened up the finances and what Yahweh needed to do in this Church.

59

Within us are the mountains and the seat of rest we are sitting on - this governing mountain - is now governing all our mountains. We must sit on each mountain and govern them. Our mountain, our seat of rest and our government moves with us and over us. When someone looks at me they will see the whole mountain of government that sits within me. When I speak others recognize the authority and government that is in and on my mountain. We need to exercise that government and that seat of rest in the midst of turmoil because when we're in rest they're in rest, the earth turns to us and it becomes a restful situation. The seat we sit on acts like a magnet and attracts God's provision to the mountain and into our life which is why we have to deal with what is on the mountain so that it can attract the provision.

Financial flow comes from that positional seat, not from individuals, so if you don't have financial flow it means you have not learned how to govern the seats. Someone said to me they could find provision and abundance in food and other areas, but they could not find the abundance in buying a new car. This person is learning how to govern in a particular seat.

Poverty is a spirit and a mindset which can be activated in us through cellular memory. My husband used to say he could believe God to travel the world but still struggled with the generational familiar spirit of poverty. I'm busy doing memoirs of the crazy stuff we did, how we travelled the world with no money and how I started five kindergartens without any finances and how God provided. He said it was a mindset that was on the inside of him that constantly spoke poverty and not to spend money and to be careful, but he was the most generous person! He used to look at the Church account and comment that it wasn't a savings account and we needed to be spending the money on the poor, widows and orphans and feeding the refugees. God always provided but there was something on the inside of him that would fight with him and say we shouldn't be spending all this money. The familiar spirits had come down generationally and always tried to speak to him. The right hand was giving but the left hand was fighting and saying, "No!" There was an unredeemed mountain that he had to fight for and sit on all the time so he could get on top of the poverty mindset.

Each mountain has a government seat which carries a blueprint which will be the operational manual that we use to operate with in every mountain. **Luke 17:21b** says, "Nor will they say, 'See here!' or 'See there!' For indeed, the kingdom of God is within you."

We need to be trained by God to be kings, priests, legislators, and oracles because when we start functioning as a king we govern everything around us. As a priest we take it before Yahweh, then we begin to legislate it and speak it out and then as an oracle we pull it from the future and land it in the present. When that happens it all begins to come out of our seat of rest. Remember that if we've lost our joy, we've lost everything.

When we're in that place we need to yield to it which means we surrender and empower the desire in us which gives us the power to govern. From my government seat (government of a country) I've been able to govern certain things with my teams in a few countries and in one particular country I was able to govern the finances because Yahweh gave me the right to govern for that nation. It was a poor country, the finances were crashing, which means the poor would have gotten poorer. We began to govern on our seat with our blueprint. We had already sat on that seat and were operating in our seat of rest on top of the seat of the mountain of government of finances for this nation. Yahweh gave us a figure that we could take their currency to; when I went into the courts of the kings, Melchizedek was there and he gave us a figure and said we could not take it lower than 16:1 to the British Pound.

In the realms of the Kingdom I saw it differently to how it is in the stock exchange and the graph was going up in a zigzag fashion because normally it would be going down. From my seat, I reached out and grabbed the graph and began to pull it down from my seat of government. Within nine months, the finances of this particular country had come down to 16:1 to the pound. It stayed at that rate and fluctuated between 16:1 and 17:1 for about two or three years and then we had COVID and it began to go up again. I went to Melchizedek and I said, "Sir, I need to know why this index is rising." He said, "You stopped governing it, Lindi. You patted yourself on the back and walked out and stopped governing."

When we govern from our seat, we need to stay governing because that's our job, to sit and govern! I just love currency, I'll speak to Yahweh about it, I'll go online to see where it's sitting on the index and govern it to where it should be because it's my job. During COVID the rate worsened and I asked Yahweh what to do so I could govern this currency properly for the sake of the nation and the poor and He gave me permission to govern it at 19:1 to the British Pound. I did that and legislated it as a king and priest and as an oracle as I pulled it from the future and into the present. Three years ago, this nation's currency was the best performing currency in the world. It wasn't the best currency, but the best performing one and recently it was again voted the best performing currency in the world. Why is this? It's a poor country. It's because someone sat on their seat, heard what was going on with the people, took the blueprint, handled the finances, stabilized it and the country refuses to crash economically. That's what sitting on our seat does. I trade on this because I want this type of responsibility.

I want to sit on my different seats and govern. My team and I went into another country's Parliamentary Buildings where Yahweh gave us the right to deal into a particular area, which was morality. We didn't have jurisdiction over their policies but only over the morality in government. We asked the Father to expose and shout morality from the roof top.

How do I know I was given this right to govern? When I was in my new home in England, the oracles were meeting on a Monday morning at 10:00 a.m., praying in tongues, speaking over Estonia and other places. I asked if anyone knew who the local MP was because I wanted to go into the Houses of Parliament in England. No one knew who the MP was. On Wednesday I was getting ready for my trip around the country to visit with the Hubs when I heard a letter come through the letter box. It was an embossed letter from the House of Commons, from our MP, inviting me to get to know her and to have a tour of Parliament!

About two years later I received another letter and this was from the Speaker of the House of Parliament inviting me to come in with our group and see what they were doing. It got to the point where I was able to vote in the English Parliamentary elections before I was a citizen of the Nation. The other people who were staying in my house, who were also getting citizenship, were not allowed to vote but for some reason I was put on the voter's role!

Yahweh was trying to show me something because my seat allows me to have authority and allows me to step into the realms of the Kingdom to begin to operate from that seat of rest as a king, a priest, a legislator, and an oracle. It's time for maturity. Finances and provision flow into these seats. The provision to go to Parliament came in along with the letter to give me permission. Desire is the key. We must have a desire to see our mountain so we can sit on it and govern from it. Desire births a dream and the dream becomes a magnet that pulls the mountain towards us.

If we are struggling with our children we can ask Yahweh to show us the mountain of our family. We can sit on this mountain, kill anything that's on it and sit on the governmental seat of rest within the mountain of our family. We can take each of our children and place them in the spirit, inside our mountain. We can hold their scrolls and their purposes and any prophetic words over them in our heart within our mountain. Scripture asks in **Psalm 24:3-4**, "Who may ascend into the hill of the Lord? Or who may stand in His holy place? He who has clean hands and a pure heart, who has not lifted up his soul to an idol, nor sworn deceitfully."

We can go into the mountain to the places where we store our scrolls and victories and other things or we can put them inside the garden of our heart or trade them on the Sea of Glass. The reason we trade on the Sea of Glass is for more revelation. Remember that our desire attracts, like a magnet, dreams and visions to it. As I hold my children in my heart it will attract the fulness of what Yahweh has for them into their own mountains.

We should already have a mountain of government, whether we've seen it or not, over our home. When we relocate we must pack up our mountain inside of our hearts and take it with us along with the angelic structures and everything we've developed within our prophetic times, prayer times, sleep times, and engaging times. When we move into the new home we must unpack our mountain, pull out everything from our heart and begin to operate in our new home. Our mountain attracts our vision and scroll and everything it needs. Sometimes people don't seem to settle because they've not moved their mountain to their new home.

In England I moved homes and I kept looking at my old house thinking it looked so lovely. I was really struggling in my new home until I realized that I hadn't moved my mountain. I drove to the old house and sat outside in my car. I packed up my mountain, the angelic structures, and all the encounters that had taken place there and put it all in my heart. I blessed the house and went back to my new home where I unpacked my mountain and it all settled. I went back to the old house to collect some mail and it looked so empty. It had no heart and soul. Prosperity was attracted to my mountain wherever I unpacked it. Plants would grow and the gardens would be beautiful. Every time I'd leave a home the owners would comment that I left the house in a better condition than how I'd received it. It's because of the mountain of government that sat over my house, along with the encounters people had and the whirlwinds that would open up above folk when they were sleeping. Someone was sleeping in my bedroom and all they could hear was a whirring noise. I had a sign with the Yod Hey Shin Vav Hey above my bed and a picture of the tree of life at the foot of my bed and they were able to see all my encounters and what I had been engaging with.

Sometimes there will be people trying to position their mountain on top of our mountain so we need to learn how to govern well. I had to learn how to go into the spirit with someone once and to tell them I had enough of what they were doing and I warned them that if they didn't stop I would have to deal with them in the spirit. I told them to move away from my mountain and to stop trying to govern it and overshadow it. They left me immediately and even blocked me on Facebook and wouldn't speak to me after that. All this happened in the spirit. We sit as kings, so others can't come and overshadow our mountain.

When we are sitting over a business, our mountain comes with us into our business and attracts finances. It might not be our own business so our blessing goes to this company and not necessarily to ourself. Grant Mahoney often says we should start something small so we can unpack our mountain of business because it has a blueprint and a magnet that attracts finances and provision.

That's why we love trading and giving because when we trade we trade into the concept of our financial mountain. I also trade into my family mountain because I'm calling them into salvation. I'm calling good, godly spouses in for them. I'm calling beautiful children in for them. I'm calling in businesses for them. In **Psalm 37:25** Scripture says, "I have been young, and now am old; yet I have not seen the righteous forsaken, nor his descendants begging bread." I'm a widow saying, "Father, I will trade because I've never been forsaken, you've shown me what it's like for You to be my husband." I trade into every mountain that I find because I want some of the truth that is in that mountain, and in doing so, intent and desire attract provision into my mountain so I can build a family dynasty.

We have the House of Masters family dynasty and have drawn our own crest because we want to develop an inheritance for generations to come. I don't want my granddaughter to come to me and say she has to go and study and then find a job. Instead I want her to tell me what she's studying so we can create a job for her and set it up so she can work and create jobs for other people. I don't want us to have to keep on battling because of family curses from freemasonry and broken mountains. So many people build up a mountain and lose it, over and over, so every generation has to try and rebuild these mountains. I want us to have a continual flow of government on the mountain of our family.

SECOND ACTIVATION

Step through the gateway of the imagination and look on the inside of you. You can place your hands on your *tiferet* if you want to. Out of your belly shall flow streams of living water. Inside of you sits the seat of rest. You are seated with Christ and have stepped through the veil of His flesh, which is the new and living way, by which you enter the Throne of Grace. Walk boldly up to the throne and ask for grace and mercy to help you in your time of need. This new covenant is written in His blood. Engage with Him and breathe Him in by looking face to face, eye to eye, nose to nose, mouth to mouth.

Breathe in and out.
Breathe in and hold, and out.
Yod Hey Vav Hey.
Breathe in His name – YAHWEH.
Breathe out His name – YAHWEH.

Bring yourself to the place of rest on the inside of you and build a mountain by taking earth or brick and place it on the inside of you. On the top of the mountain I want you to see a throne. Sit on it and if there's a dragon, cut off its head, legs and tail, slit open its belly and take out the treasures that are there and place them on the inside of you.

Yahweh, we sit seated with Christ in heavenly places engaging with the fulness of Yeshua haMashiach, our physical and carnal bodies are now arcing with our spiritual body and we see ourselves seated in Christ in heavenly places.

Yod Hey Vav Hey.

See the seat of rest and see rest flowing in you as you govern from this place of rest. Breathe in the peace of Yahweh, because He is the Prince of Peace. You govern from this place of peace and because of that you begin to attract peace to yourself. In the midst of turmoil, you sit in peace and rest on the inside of your belly.

I've begun to calm the upper and the lower waters so that chaos becomes balanced. The chaos of the lower waters through the earth and the *malkuth* is coming up through me and creating balance and the *Mem*, instead of becoming chaotic, becomes balanced.

Yod Hey Vav Hey.

From this place you can take all the treasures, scrolls, promises and prophetic words and place them on the inside of your mountain and govern from that place. If you want to do that for your children then grow a mountain, pull it together, sit on top of the seat of rest on top of the government mountain for your family and your children and call them in from the north, south, east, and west and put them into your mountain. Put the promises of God for your children into the mountain.

Father, we thank You for salvation and for healing. Some of them want to fall pregnant, for financial freedom, for jobs, for deliverance. Some of you have children who have chosen a path that you're not comfortable with and you know it's not Yahweh's plan and provision for them so we pull in the truth of who they are from Zion. Say to your children, "Remember your way back to Zion. Remember who you are. Remember why you came through the *mazzeroth*." We're moving and operating from a seat of rest, not a seat of panic.

Yod, Hey, Vav, Hey.

Some of you feel you need to wrap up your mountain over your old place of abode or business. I want you to look at that place in the spirit, remember what it looks like, take the mountain and pack it up into your heart. Come to your current place of abode/ work and unpack the mountain over your head, sit on top of it, let the blueprint come out and attract provision to this mountain. We honour the one we've left but we honour the one we're in. We have angelic hosts that sit on this mountain and we begin to let whatever is necessary to be attracted to the mountain.

Today Father, we thank You that we are constantly aware that out of our belly flows rivers of living water. As I sit on my seat of government and my seat of rest on the inside of me, I choose to remember that I'm always seated there, governing from this mountain as I begin to operate as a mature son in Yahweh.

I want to encourage you to draw your mountains or write down what they are and what they do. Write down the prophetic words and the promises, sit on your seats on each mountain and govern over your mountain.

This is a time of maturity.

Chapter 5
Beholding The Body

We must sit within our mountain and ask Yahweh to establish certain things within our life. These engagements are for everyone to participate in and if we know who we are, understand the process, and begin to walk this out, we will see amazing things unfold.

As your mountain has been unfolded and you have engaged with it, an activation has started to take place within you. I may deliver one teaching but it might have several assignments: teaching, activation, or discovery. The assignment for these teachings is to activate your ability to see your position as a son and to see these things unfold.

One of the greatest issues I see within the lives of individuals is insecurity. This manifests itself when we are about to have imminent breakthrough and about to enter into being secure in our identity, in the establishment of who we are created to be in creation. Insecurity will become a damper over the things we should be engaging with and walking out. We must sit over those insecurities, govern them, bring them into calibration, and get them judged by going to the Mobile Court so that the record of the negative effect gets judged and we start stepping into the truth that sets us free. We must not complicate the simplicity of the Kingdom.

I had an encounter several years ago while I was asking questions about who I was. There are so many things sitting on the inside of us and hearing someone else's story is good, but we need to get to a place where we can engage with this for ourselves. I started to yearn, through desire, to begin to unlock some things within me. I was standing in the front of the hall during a time of worship, there were dancers in the front and a lot of activity happening around me. I was engaging with the teaching in my heart that I was going to share after worship was finished and suddenly the sound of worship and the dancers faded away and I stood in silence engaging and beholding this image that was appearing in front of me. When something shifts into my vision, I honour and behold it because I know something is going to unfold.

The more I engaged with the image the clearer it became and in front of me stood a man. The atmosphere shifted around him and through cardiognosis (knowledge of the heart) I knew that this was Jacob. He is such a fascinating person that he will transform and change you if you get a chance to engage with him. He is different to how Scripture makes him out to be. I then saw a menorah which turned on its side, penetrating his being. During this encounter there were many significant details locked into the record of my memory. I watched the menorah inside of him turning into this vibrating, electric, blue flame and the seven Realms of the Kingdom opened up.

Prior to my encounter with Jacob I had been fascinated with the menorah and the seven Realms of the Kingdom and had been pursuing these through reading the Word and other literature. I had been engaging with my studies and arcing with the books I was reading and then this encounter started to unfold. As I was engaging with Jacob he started to fade away and come back, every time he faded I would see an image of myself, as in a mirror, become clearer every time he faded. The same menorah with the seven Realms of the Kingdom, which was positioned in Jacob, was positioned within me. He was reflecting what was happening within him and showing it in me. I was looking at myself and couldn't comprehend, at that stage of my pursuit, that the Realms of the Kingdom of Yahweh were being positioned in me.

My pursuit and my desire, saying to Yahweh that I needed to understand who I was, unlocked something for me. Jacob knew he had the answer to that question and through an encounter could say to me, "Rick, I want to show you who you are." That's how the Kingdom of Yahweh operates, through desire, where we position ourselves in that place so whatever we have a heart for we set ourselves in motion to engage with people who are in the Kingdom, whether they are saints of old, the cloud of witnesses, the twenty-four elders, Beings or the angelic. This creates an atmosphere for us to see what is going to respond because of our desire.

In **Genesis 28:10-13** Scripture says the following, "Now Jacob went out from Beersheba and went toward Haran. So he came to a certain place and stayed there all night, because the sun had set. And he took one of the stones of that place and put it at his head, and he lay down in that place to sleep. Then he dreamed, and behold, a ladder was set up on the earth, and its top reached to heaven; and there the angels of God were ascending and descending on it. And behold, the Lord stood above it and said: 'I am the Lord God of Abraham your father and the God of Isaac; the land on which you lie I will give to you and your descendants.'"

When we read in **Genesis 1** that 'Yahweh said' we frame it through the English language so we read it as it is, but how could Yahweh have said what He said if there was no language at that time? How did Yahweh speak? When He created the heavens and the earth He did not look over it and say, "Let there be light" in English. He created the living letters so that they could, through Yahweh's thought and desire, release a frequency into creation so that things began to manifest. In the same way, our thoughts, desires and our connection and union with Yahweh should activate something in us to begin to create around us, not just by what we say but what we think through the framework to create. This is powerful.

Some people have said they prefer the grace of Yahweh because we're under grace and not under law. Within the law, it is written that if we commit adultery, it's a sin. When we look at grace we think we can do what we want. We say that once we are saved we are always saved, but Yeshua explained grace in this way: He understands we don't want to be under the law anymore because of what He did, so now grace is this; if we think or look at someone in a lustful way, it is a sin and as though we have committed adultery. The question is, what do we want? Law or grace?

When we understand what happened with Jacob and the framework that Yahweh was speaking into Jacob, it was being established from within him to establish something without. **Genesis 28:16-17**, "Then Jacob awoke from his sleep and said, 'Surely the Lord is in this place, and I did not know it.' And he was afraid and said, 'How awesome is this place! This is none other than the house of God, and this is the gate of heaven.'"

We know that Jacob rested in an open field for the night where he took one of the stones to rest his head on. There was no building, so when he said that the place was an awesome house and gate, he understood the encounter and I realized through his encounter and my walk with him that when he took one of the stones it wasn't what we think it is. In my pursuit and engagement and going in, I found out that 'stone' means portal or gateway.

Jacob rested his head, not his physical head but his place of government, within the mountain of who he was, through one of the gateways, because Scripture says he took one of the stones to rest his head upon to engage and encounter with the Kingdom Realms that were positioned within. When he had the encounter he said, "This is no other than the house of God," which was himself. He was the gate and the transition point of heaven. The house houses all things that are in the Kingdom, positioned within us. The gate or transition point are the twenty gates positioned within us and are seated in creation, they have a massive impact in who we are becoming as a son.

I realized that what was happening in Jacob was framing the law of first mention about what 'house' and 'gate' mean. Subconsciously I had believed that the house mentioned in Jacob's encounter was the Church that we would go to and the gate was the Church entrance. This is not what Scripture speaks about in terms of the house of God. When 'house' is mentioned it is talking about sons understanding what is happening within.

During my encounter with Jacob I realized that the menorah was positioned within me and the seven Realms of the Kingdom were within me. This changed my life completely. When we engage with an encounter to that degree and step into it, what we behold we become. I could now sit within that place and discover each Kingdom that Yahweh had allowed to be positioned within me.

THE SEVEN REALMS OF THE KINGDOM

The Kingdom of the Earth
The Kingdom of God
The Kingdom of Heaven
Heaven
Heaven of Heavens

Perfection
Eternity

These seven Realms of the Kingdom are connected to the menorah and to us and flow through the gates of the spirit, soul, and body with our position as a being in creation. Whatever is happening within us, as we go in and out to behold, that transformation is transforming us so when we walk in creation, what has happened in that realm is affecting things in our earthly realm. That is why Yeshua said in **Matthew 7:16a**, "You will know them by their fruits."

Fruit is the physical manifestation of our spiritual pursuit. That is how I measure my journey. I don't talk about things that I do in the spirit until I have fruit attached to it because then it has the backing of heaven and when I speak, it's from a place of testimony, giving people an opportunity to step into it as well. I don't talk about things from a place of knowledge. If I were to listen to Lindi's encounters and teachings and just relay her message through knowledge because they are good teachings, without having become it, it's no good. We must become the revelation, so I only teach on what I've seen the fruit of in my own life. Daily I go in and behold and I see things shift and a transformation taking place. Recently something significant happened in the Kingdom Realms that brought about a massive impact in my life, but I have not yet seen the fruit so I will not speak about it.

Kingdom of the Earth

When I started to understand that the Realms of the Kingdom are within me, I realized there was a process I needed to go through to go into the Kingdoms Realm. I started off by establishing the Kingdom I wanted to be positioned in which is the Kingdom of the Earth. Many Christians are caught up within this Kingdom, which is an amazing place with two gates, one being the gate that we can access to go beyond the Kingdom of the Earth, which is the gate of Yeshua. Scripture says in **Hebrews 10:19-20**, "Therefore, brethren, having boldness to enter the Holiest by the blood of Jesus, by a new and living way which He consecrated for us, through the veil, that is, His flesh." The other gate looks like the first but is a counterfeit gate leading to a counterfeit realm apart from Yeshua. If we engage with Yeshua through an encounter, and are positioned within Him, unlocking the spiritual man that we are, which is the new creature, we can access the other realms.

Christians that are deeply connected to the religious structure backed by the religious spirit will have that gate blocked by that spirit so that they will not behold all the other Kingdom Realms, which should be their portion but because of the trade, cannot access it. The Kingdom of the Earth has the spiritual world and the natural world. These worlds co-exist and we are positioned in their midst. What happens spiritually within the Kingdom of the Earth will affect the natural realm, both negatively and positively. If we see negative things manifest within the earth, a trade would have taken place spiritually but still within the Kingdom of the Earth, to affect things negatively within the natural.

What we do as sons, seated within our rightful position, and engage, behold, legislate, and pray in the Spirit, has an impact within creation and within the natural. As sons, we understand that we are positioned within the earth, yet we keep connection and intimacy with the Kingdom Realms positioned within us so we can go and behold what is our portion that brings a massive impact within the Kingdom of the Earth. As sons we go beyond the Kingdom of the Earth.

Kingdom of God

The second Kingdom Realm that I engaged with is the Kingdom of God. It is the functionality of a realm that can only flow through us if we've been there because we can only release a Kingdom which we live from. Within the narrow mindset of the Church Age we've been taught that there is Heaven and hell. We live here on earth trusting for the rapture and one day when we die, we will be with Jesus in Heaven. Which part of Heaven is that? Have we been there? Have we engaged? The Kingdom of God is above the Kingdom of the Earth and when we access that as a son we begin to understand that, as a function of our seat in the Kingdom, we operate in authority which brings about transformation. Within this Kingdom Realm we will also see the function of the gifts.

The gifts we see manifest in the Church Age were given to the Church in its immaturity as gateways for them to step into a far greater dimension to access it to become it. When operating as a son from this place, we are not relying on the gifts to rest upon us through Yahweh's grace but we go in to learn how the gifts operate so that we can *become the gifts in creation*, not relying on grace, but as a son being transformed by what it is doing in us.

There was a time in my life when I was relying on the gift of healing to bring about healing in those around me. I relied on Yahweh's grace because there was no work I was doing to obtain this gift. The gift I was working in was not being allowed to become a gateway within me so I could behold it in order to become it so that it could transform my life and then those around me. I was on this side of the veil and I started to use the gift to heal people so that they could look at the gift sitting on me so that they needed me there physically otherwise they would not get healed. That was immature. Being immature means we

77

function in these gifts by being positioned in the Kingdom of God but operating under the grace extended to us from Yahweh. There is an expression of government on our life when we operate within this realm as a mature son, not just relying on the gifts.

I started to go in, behold, see, and engage, and through this process I would feel something shift within me. When I would come out and walk upon the earth I would do things and see the fruit. Then I knew that what had transformed me there was transforming me here in creation.

The Kingdom of Heaven

Next, I engaged with the Kingdom of Heaven. This is not the Heaven we have been taught about and think we know. This is the manifestation of a realm which comes upon us and is where we will see signs and wonders. This is not the same as the signs and wonders manifesting on the Kingdom of the Earth through the giftings but because of the government of the Kingdom of heaven sitting upon us, we are able to manifest things in creation. A sign and a wonder takes place where it's not about us being framed as the one who has brought about the sign, but it's when creation doesn't know what happened but knows something happened. Sometimes we're in a conference and there is something happening and we know that creation is responding to a sign that is echoing through creation that everyone is fully aware of. It's a sign resting on us which reflects the government of the Kingdom of Heaven.

In this realm we will have dominion over creation and it will respond to us by drawing itself closer to us because of what is sitting on us. My wife operates within the Kingdom of Heaven and creation responds to her. We were at the aquarium by a tank holding a large fish called a Grouper. Some visitors were talking about the Grouper and there was a photograph of the fish above the tank. It was hiding behind a rock so the tank looked empty. Melanie stepped up to the glass and out of the blue appeared the Grouper from behind the rock. It started to show itself off in front of my wife because of the government of the Kingdom of Heaven sitting over her, so the fish came out to behold what was happening within her. That is the function of government that we carry. We should be able to walk out and creation responds to us because of the government sitting within us as a son.

Heaven

Heaven is where Yahweh sits in absolute dominion on His throne. This is where Yahweh's Mountain sits. Even though some of us have no idea what we're doing, but the intent of our heart is wanting to learn and engage, He will allow us to go from the Kingdom of the Earth and all of a sudden we begin to engage with His mountain that is positioned within Heaven and we look at that place and go, "Wow!" as we've literally gone through three realms to get to the place where Yahweh is establishing something for us. Seeing Yahweh's Mountain should transform us. This is where the Mountain of the Lord sits and is also called Mount Zion.

When we engage with this process, Yahweh will unfold His amazing Mountain. In my pursuit, this Mountain started to arc with Moshe (Moses) who went up and into the Mountain of Yahweh. When I beheld what happened within that encounter with Moshe I saw the Nation of Israel and saw the fear that they had because they saw Moshe go up and in. Not only did I see Moshe go into the Mountain but I saw the Mountain lift off the ground! Within this encounter, the Nation of Israel saw daylight come through from under the mountain as Moshe stepped in and went up because it was the Mountain of the Lord. In that place he engaged with Yahweh and came out of the Mountain looking 'other.' Scripture is not just words written on a page. Sometimes the way the Bible is written is not in its original form which is why we must read it by the Spirit.

If we read Scripture and see that something we've been taught has been omitted, it will be in the Kingdom and we just need to go through to behold. Sons must take the time to sit and engage with Scripture, not religiously, but going in and through by the Spirit.

There are no words in our languages to frame the encounter that Moshe had when he came out looking 'other.' The same thing happened to Yeshua on the Mount of Transfiguration and the Word says that His face became 'other.' I watched what was unfolding and I realized that within Heaven is where Yahweh's Mountain sits and we can go in to behold these things that are unfolding for us. We can access the chambers that are inside that Mountain and gain access to the things there that are for us to bring about a transformation. Because of our position as a son we can go in there. We are no longer servants. In **John 15:15** Yeshua said, "No longer do I call you servants, for a servant does not know what his master is doing; but I have called you friends, for all things that I heard from My Father I have made known to you." But not only friends, He also calls us sons, so we can go in and behold. We have the access point! We have been taught differently and now have to train ourselves and untangle ourselves from what we've been taught so we can go there.

We will never inherit the fullness of the Kingdom if our framework is dwelling on the shortcomings we are dealing with. We must make a conscious decision to step completely into the fullness regardless of what we believe and what is warring against what we are learning. The price was paid at Calvary when Yeshua became the access point for us so this can become our reality. We read in **Revelation 4:1**, "After these things I looked, and behold, a door standing open in heaven, and the first voice which I had heard, like the sound of a trumpet speaking with me, said, 'Come up here and I will show you what must take place after these things.'" John received an invitation to come up higher and if we want to have a glimpse of what is around the throne within Heaven, where Yahweh's Mountain sits, we can read **Revelation 4**. It gives us an access point to see what we can find there.

When we go through the Kingdom Realms that are sitting within us, and enter Heaven, and behold what is there I believe the journey starts from that point. The function of the other realms below Heaven are amazing and the government we can carry is amazing but when we enter the realms of Heaven and start bearing the image of our Father, that's where the transformation will happen. The same thing happened to Moshe. When he got there his countenance changed through transfiguration.

Heaven of Heavens

Paul speaks about the spiritual bodies which are our portion, and we know we have the five different bodies we engage with which unlocks the sixth body which is called the god-body or the god-man. Paul spoke about what was on the earth and what was in the Kingdom and he said that when we enter into the Heaven of Heavens we become displayed to the celestial arena which means our celestial body has become unveiled so we can begin to govern in that place. While engaging in an encounter, Yahweh turned my physical being toward my celestial being and I began to see it before I came back out because I saw the authority and responsibility that I felt within that arena. Yahweh allowed me to glance in so I could behold my responsibility, but I was fully aware I still needed to work on aspects here so when I get there I have the maturity to begin to establish things.

When we engage within these realms that transform us, we want to hold them so dear to our heart that we will not display it all on social media for the world to see. The more we understand the responsibility, the more we want Yahweh to get the glory and for us to remain in the place of hiddenness.

In **Deuteronomy 10:14** we read, "Behold, to the Lord your God belong heaven and the highest heavens, the earth and all that is in it."

All these things interact together and are seated together. **Psalm 148:4** says. "Praise Him highest heavens, and the waters that are above the heavens."

Psalm 68:33, "To Him who rides upon the highest heavens, which are from ancient times; behold He speaks forth with His voice, a mighty voice."

The Heaven of Heavens is there for us to step into to behold, within the Kingdom Realms that are positioned inside of us.

Perfection

The Kingdom of Perfection is where our DNA begins to be transformed which comes through intimacy when we are seated within the place of perfection.

I go in and go through. I behold and see what Yahweh is unfolding for me which begins to impact me spiritually so that I hold its record and I begin to establish it within the record of the being that I am. It goes through the twenty gates and when I'm seated in Creation I begin to administrate what I have become. Everything around me should respond because of the transformation and transfiguration that is happening there.

Eternity

The Kingdom of Eternity is where the likes of Enoch are. He walked and was no more. Elijah began to go up there. Moshe came back from there to pick up his body and take it back into the Kingdom Realms. Scripture records four people that have their physical body, Yeshua, Enoch, Moshe, and Elijah. Moshe and Elijah came **through Yeshua** on the mount of transfiguration and the disciples asked if they could build three homes, one for each of them. If Moshe and Elijah did not have their physical body there would have been no need for building them a shelter.

When we honour ourselves within the process and this journey we will begin to arc with so much more that is our portion. We must sit in it and behold, engage, and understand the transformation happening within us.

Because of the times we are living in, it is imperative to know who we are and to deal with the inconsistencies of our thought process that speaks anything other than what Yahweh has spoken about us within Creation.

Chapter 6
Accessing The Body

Proverbs 11:30a says, "The fruit of the righteous is a tree of life."

P'ri tzadik ets chay פרי צדיק עץ חיים

We are trees of righteousness planted by the Lord.

Ets (male noun, to be firm) = TREE and is written with the Hebrew letters ע צ
Chay (a living thing) = LIFE and is written with the Hebrew letters י ח

These two words mean the following: The eye to watch the desire, to separate, to look at the hand of Yahweh on the inside of us.

Ets chay can be translated to mean a firm and living thing.

The fruit of the righteous is a firm and living thing on the inside of us - the Tree of Life.

The Tree of Life
Sefirot

I like to engage with all the points on the Tree of Life because they're also connected to our health. The emanations of Wisdom and Understanding are placed on either side of our head and when they talk to us, Knowledge, which is in the area of our thyroid, will hear what Wisdom is saying and will understand it so it becomes knowledge in our body. When we don't want to take all the information we know which will take us into maturity, when we're stubborn and hide behind our issues and we refuse to deal with them, often our thyroid will manifest. If I hear a sound in my right ear, I will ask Wisdom what she's trying to say so I can use my left side which is where Understanding is so it can become knowledge which works its way through my body.

We are going to activate the Tree of Life, the ets chay inside of us, so we can get the points to operate. The Bible says that the government of God sat on Yeshua's shoulders. When we look at the picture of the Tree of Life, we see Loving-kindness on the right shoulder and Judgment and Justice on the left. The words justice and righteousness are the same word in Hebrew. The four pillars of love are made up of justice, judgment, grace, and mercy or loving-kindness. The Scripture is saying that the government is made up of the four pillars which are justice, judgment, grace, and mercy which is the *ets chay*, the Tree of Life on the inside of Yeshua, the firm and living thing that sits on the inside of all of us.

Point 1 - Crown
The crown is a gate on the top of our heads. Scripture says in **Psalm 24:7-8**, "Lift up your heads, O you gates! And be lifted up, you everlasting doors! And the King of glory shall come in. Who is this King of glory? The Lord strong and mighty, The Lord mighty in battle."

Point 2 - Wisdom
Wisdom is placed on the right side of our bodies which is connected to our intellect.

Point 3 – Understanding
This is placed on the left side and is connected to the angel Tzadkiel.

Point 4 – Grace and Mercy

In Hebrew the word is *chesed*. Michael the Archangel is connected to grace, mercy and lovingkindness. This point arcs with day one of creation.

Point 5 – Justice and Judgment

Gevurah is connected to the North within my body which is the gate through which justice and righteousness come and arcs with day two of creation.

Point 6 – Glory

This is the seat of our emotion and Scripture says in **John 7:38**, "He who believes in Me, as the Scripture has said, out of his heart will flow rivers of living water." The upper waters are above this point and the lower waters are below this point. This point in the Tree of Life brings balance. At times we will feel some chaos in our emotional seat so we need to be sitting on our seat of rest on the inside of us. This point arcs with the third day of creation as well as being the point which brings balance.

Point 7 – Victory

This is also the place of endurance. Sometimes people struggle with their hips because they might have had a mighty battle in the area of endurance and victory which could result in a physical manifestation in our body and arcs with day four of creation.

Point 8 - Splendour and Awe

The shining light of Yahweh and arcs with the fifth day of creation.

Point 9 – Foundation

This is where we find divine creativity and the area of fertility which arcs with day six of creation when man was made. We have the *ets chay*, the Tree of Life, within us and there is also the Tree of the Knowledge of Good and Evil. When our emotions stir up within the area of divine creativity, sexual hormones stir up. In the Church Age we taught our young people that these hormones and desires were evil and they shouldn't be engaging with these feelings. We now know there are two trees within the one tree; one side is the Tree of Life and the other side is the Tree of the Knowledge of Good and Evil. If, as a Church, we were taught to direct those urges from our foundation area into the Tree of Life and into divine creativity, we would not be in so much trouble when it comes to sexual immorality. Instead, we have pushed into the Tree of the Knowledge of Good and Evil which results in pornography and immorality because it needs an outworking and ends in shame.

If we had taught people to direct that emotion and the energy to that foundation area of creativity we would have known how to direct that creative energy into the ets chay, the Tree of Life, that would have enabled us to be amazingly creative. If you are creative in any area – painting, drawing, dancing, writing, coding, and business, this is when you are using the energy that is created in this area and direct it into the Tree of Life.

I have a ministry friend who told me that when he would be stirred up in this area he would take that energy and channel it into creating new businesses and developing ideas. Instead of this having an outworking in sexual immorality we can divert our attention by speaking in tongues and concentrating on a divine outworking in creativity.

Point 10 – Rest

This is the area of the sword, the crown of righteousness, the sceptre of Yahweh and is connected into the earth. In Hebrew, this area is called the *malkuth*. Creation is groaning and waiting to be manifest through the *malkuth* into the body, up into the upper waters, to take what we see in the mysteries of Yahweh and the secrets of Yahweh in the *choshek*, to bring it down through the body, through the *malkuth* and back into the earth and arcs with the seventh day of creation.

This briefly sums up the *ets chay*, the Tree of Life, the firm and living thing on the inside of us. Each area is an ascension point which we can engage with. The twenty-two living letters are also placed on the inside of us which are gateways to the Kingdom Realms and together with the ten activation points give us the thirty-two pathways of Wisdom.

For example, *Alef* א is near our lungs, so every time we breathe, we are activating this living letter within us. If we are battling to sleep, we can engage with the letter *Samekh* ס which is placed on the left hip between splendour and divine creativity because *Samekh* gives us sleep. We can ask him what we need to deal into on this side of our body in order to fix sleeplessness because God gives His beloved rest.

Shin, *Alef* and *Mem* are called the three mothers and represent the elements of fire, air, and water.

Shin – fire – ש
Alef – air – א
Mem – water – מ
The menorah also sits on the inside of us and each arm represents one of the seven Kingdom Realms:

Kingdom of the Earth
Kingdom of God
Kingdom of Heaven
Heaven
Heaven of Heavens
Perfection

Eternity

The seven Spirits of Yahweh are also on the Tree of Life which are mentioned in **Isaiah 11:1-3** and are:

The Spirit of the Lord
The Spirit of Wisdom
The Spirit of Understanding
The Spirit of Counsel
The Spirit of Might
The Spirit of Knowledge
The Spirit of the Fear of the Lord

All of the above move within us like an atom within our DNA as we engage with our different bodies whilst sitting on our seat of rest within our mountain.

ACTIVATION

We will engage the different points within us of the *ets chay*, so we can begin to understand our bodies, that the Tree of Life, which is an entity, lives on the inside of us and that we have a menorah that connects these points. Our DNA strand moves up and down all of this.

Righteousness means right standing with Yahweh and the fruit of this righteousness, or right standing, is the Tree of Life within us.

We will now activate this tree by arcing with it so we can feel its frequency living and moving within us.

We engage with the crown (lift up your heads o ye gates). Father, I thank you for the Tree of Life, the *ets chay* on the inside of me, the firm and living thing that is part of who I am as a

righteous one. Today I engage with the crown and I thank You for the crown.
Yod Hey Vav Hey.
I speak the name of Yahweh over my crown.
Yod Hey Vav Hey.
Lift up your head o you gates, lift up your everlasting door.
Yod Hey Vav Hey.
I want you to feel your gate opening up in that place of engagement within.

We move to our right ear. The Spirit of Wisdom doesn't live here but she speaks to us.
Yod Hey Vav Hey.
I activate the ability to hear Wisdom speak to me.

We move to our left ear where we get Understanding.
Yod Hey Vav Hey.
I open up Understanding and engage within.
Yod Hey Vav Hey.
When Wisdom speaks, I undertake to understand so I can have knowledge.

We move to the *Da'at* which is Knowledge.
Yod Hey Vav Hey.
I activate the ability in me, the Tree of Life, the ets chay, so it becomes knowledge through understanding.
Yod Hey Vav Hey.

Put your hands on your belly which is the seat of emotion.
Yod Hey Vav Hey.
Father, out of my belly flow rivers of living water.
Yod Hey Vav Hey.
This is the place of the seat of rest, where the upper and lower waters meet and the chaos is formed into balance.

Yod Hey Vav Hey.
During times when you feel uneasy and know something is wrong, find a quiet place and address your belly and speak to the rivers of living water through the place of the glory, the emotional side of you, and speak in tongues. Start speaking peace to the chaos.

We now speak to the *netzach* which is on the right hip and is the part of us that engages with Victory and Endurance. Father, I thank You for victory and I thank You that I will endure to the end. You are my victorious One and I will have victory. I activate, within the tree within me, victory and endurance.

Thank You for Splendour and Awe, *hod*, on my left hip to be activated on the *ets chay* within me, the Tree of Life. Victory is my portion and splendour and awe begin to flow through me through the *Mem* speaking within, through the waters of Yahweh. I thank you for victory and endurance and I thank You for splendour and awe.

Lay your hand on the yesod which is between your belly button and your reproductive organs. Father, I thank You for divine creativity and fertility, the foundation of who I am.
Yod Hey Vav Hey.
I activate this area. It is one of the most sought-after places on the tree by the enemy. We activate that point within us on the Tree of Life, that we can take it and bring it into divine creativity and fertility, into this place of Yahweh in the foundation of who I am, bringing it back into its original intent within. If it's being used in the wrong areas, we say, Father forgive us and we turn our attention into the correct way of using this part of the tree within. We channel that energy into divine creativity.

We now look at rest, the *malkuth*, the part that connects into the

91

earth. Father, we activate every place upon which our foot shall tread which is mentioned in **Joshua 1:3** because it's connected into the earth and You have given it to us. This is where the firm and living thing, the *ets chay* is connected into the earth. Yod Hey Vav Hey.

We honour You and bless You, Yahweh. We honour this important part of the tree which is connecting me into the earth. The whole of creation is waiting for the *malkuth* to wake up within me in the *ets chay*, the firm foundation of who I am in Yahweh, so that it begins to be a conduit of the flow of Yahweh from Heaven down into the earth. As it is in Heaven so too on the earth, **Matthew 6:10**. We activate that part of the tree on the inside of us.

A while ago we went on holiday and wanted to see elephants. The guide had never seen them close to the area where we were. My daughter and I have quoted this Scripture before in similar situations to draw the goodness of Yahweh to us like a magnet and it says in **Isaiah 60:1-3**, "Arise, shine; for your light has come! And the glory of the Lord has risen upon you. For behold, darkness (*choshek* = mystery) shall cover the earth, and deep darkness the people; but the Lord will arise over you, and His glory will be seen upon you. The Gentiles shall come to your light, and kings to the brightness of your arising." We were able to apply this Scripture because we've activated this tree on the inside of us so it draws things to us like a magnet.

I spoke to my daughter and told her I wanted to see elephants so we decided to do this and pray and ask them to come to the light of our shining. I didn't have to do this by faith because I'm so aware of the menorah and the tree sitting within me and I expect things to be drawn to the light of my shining. I expect things to find me. After we prayed we carried on with our tour and saw a lot of hippos and crocodiles and fish eagles. As we were coming to the end of our two-hour tour and were heading back, my son exclaimed, "Look! An elephant!" The guide was so excited he decided we weren't going back as he'd never seen one in that area in the ten years he had been working there.

The next evening we were in the same town eating dinner. After supper we noticed that three hippopotamuses had come out of the river and were walking through town to graze grass in the park. The locals we were with had never seen that before. Because I know the menorah is within me and I know the Tree of the Life is within me, I was able to call the animals to the light of my shining as I put my feet, my *malkuth*, into the earth.

We can do that with gold and silver and business deals and even the right life partner as we begin to be aware of what sits within us. The tree within us glows with wisdom, understanding, knowledge, justice and judgment, mercy and grace, emotions and glory, victory and splendour, divine creativity, and the rest of Yahweh.

I've seen this work in many areas of my life. We bought a broken property and after a while the neighbour's trees started growing over and under our fence. Yeshua said that if the people would not worship Him then the trees of the field would worship Him and the rocks would cry out in worship to Him. This is what creation is waiting for and what the earth is attracted to; us to be awakened to what is within us. If we could all walk in the light of our shining because we've activated all of these points of the *ets chay* within us, that firm and living Tree of Life that is the fruit of righteousness, everything gets attracted to us without us having to do too much. It all comes and finds its place in us and looks for us and hunts us down. In **Psalm 23:6** we read, "Surely goodness and mercy shall follow me all the days of my life; and I will dwell in the house of the Lord forever."

We can imagine ourselves as trees walking around with our bodies on the inside and all the activation points responding.

The Tree of Life is also associated with ascension where we arc with the Kingdom Realms within the Tree of Life in our DNA. Once, I was laying on my bed and I saw something come out of my belly like a scene out of the Jack and the Beanstalk story. When I asked Ian what that was he said I needed to deal into my DNA. I had never seen something like this before. Jacob also had this encounter in **Genesis 28**.

There are an additional two Hebrew letters that I can now use which are the *Ghah* and the *Shin Gadol* and are ascension letters that were hidden by the Jews when their temple was destroyed. They did this so the Gentiles would not find them and use them for the wrong purpose. Using our DNA 'ladder' we can now arc from the earth into the *choshek* and back again.

I believe ascension is not going up to a place but it is engaging the natural and carnal body with the spiritual body. Ascension is not going up but looking at or arcing with. I don't ascend with my groups in the Realms of the Kingdom, I engage with my groups. If I keep saying that I'm ascending, then I keep myself in a place of constantly having to get there from the earth. I know I'm seated with Christ in heavenly places and **Proverbs 18:21** says, "Death and life are in the power of the tongue, and those who love it will eat its fruit."
So, I'm not ascending to that body, I'm arcing with that body by turning this natural body to my spiritual body and arcing. I get into agreement and engage with my bodies through the veil of His flesh into the Realms of the Kingdom and do what I must. I don't ascend in order to do anything because that would place me squarely under the sun which is the system of corruption and we're living above the system of corruption. We live on the earth

under the sun, moon, and stars but they don't govern us.

One day I was about to fly somewhere and someone told me that my zodiac sign said it was going to be a bad day for me and that I would be sick. I caught the flight anyway and as I was sitting in the plane I told the stars that they couldn't tell me what kind of day I was going to have because the Tree of Life within me governs what kind of day I will have. I cut off the soul ties between the stars and what they were trying to dictate to me and placed myself above the corrupt moral compass of man which is under the sun, the moon, and the stars.

I don't govern time. I speak to it in honour and tell it that it doesn't tell me what to do but I tell it what to do. I don't serve time because it serves me. Every number on the clock has an angel that governs that specific hour of time. Before the fall of Adam there was no time.

I'm not being disrespectful but under a corrupt system where time has been perverted, time governs. We have a saying that says, "Time is money." Time is not money and we need to repent if we say that. Money comes from the Father and hunts me down and finds me. Money comes because I'm walking as a fully-fledged, divinely created being created by Yahweh to create wealth and **Deuteronomy 8:18** says, "And you shall remember the Lord your God, for it is He who gives you power to get wealth, that He may establish His covenant which He swore to your fathers, as it is this day."

Time is not money and time serves me. Through the cube of my life I have had to step into the *olam* and speak to time to tell it that I don't serve it and that it had to slow down so I could do everything I *had* to do in the course of the day so I still had time to do the things I *wanted* to do. I have pulled time towards myself and told it that I needed to finish what I was doing and I was not going to 'run out of time.' I've learned how to operate as an *ets chay* and as a son. In **Joshua 10:12**, we read how Joshua was able to carry on fighting when Yahweh stopped the sun and to be fair, I believe *they* stopped the sun.

The *malkuth* must reflect from man and the earth, all that is above. We are a tree and we will manifest the fullness of who Yahweh is. We have a menorah within us manifesting the Kingdom of the Earth, the Kingdom of God (**Luke 17:21**), the Kingdom of Heaven, Heaven, Heaven of Heavens, Perfection and Eternity. They are all embedded in who we are. As we engage with these Realms of the Kingdom, the seven Spirits of God begin to engage with us and the seven spiritual points also engage with us as we begin to operate as a white light being. We can say, "Arise, and shine for your light has come, the glory of the Lord has risen upon you." Kings will come to the brightness of your shining. They will see this Tree of Life emanating from within us and ask us who we are.

The *choshek* is placed above the crown and is known as the dark cloud of the Lord and the place of mystery. I had an encounter where I had to go through the fiery Seraphim and I saw Yahweh's feet. It was very dark in there but the glory was so overwhelming and I remember thinking I would be happy to lie here at His feet for an eternity, basking in the immense joy and beauty. It was so gorgeous. As we reach up through the *Ghah* and the *Shin Gadol* and stretch into the *choshek*, we do the same as the priests in the temple where they would put their hook into the meat pot and pull out their meat portion for the day.

Yeshua gave the disciples this prayer, "Our Father who is in heaven, (the choshek), hallowed be Your name, Your Kingdom come, (All seven Kingdoms being activated) and Your will be done, on the earth (manifesting the Kingdom realms on Earth) as it is in Heaven. Give us today our daily bread." The priests' portion from the meat pot was just enough for that day, like the time in the wilderness when the people had quail and manna to sustain them daily. The word for manna in Hebrew is 'what is it?' The people couldn't store it because if they did it would become full of worms. They would be implying that God wouldn't provide for the next day. We must fish in the *choshek* and the daily supply of the mysteries and the glory and the intimacy with Yahweh and draw it into our lives.

We travelled as missionaries into Norway for many years and a time came when Yahweh did such unusual things because of the prevalent strong religious spirit. The Lutheran Church was the state religion and very controlling. During worship, small piles of manna would manifest and we would break bread with it. When we put it on our tongues it dissolved and tasted like sesame seeds and honey.

During this time, a lady supernaturally received gold teeth. She had previously worked as an assistant companion to the Queen's daughter and was very regal and proper. She needed dental work and I prayed for her healing. As I was praying she was saying amen and I saw something shining in her mouth. The Norwegians are so conservative so to ask them to open their mouth so someone can look inside is not done! I went to the Pastor's wife and asked her to look in the lady's mouth. They both reluctantly complied and it turned out that she had received seven gold teeth! They both screamed and the Pastor's wife fell backwards. The lady went home and shone a torch in her mouth to show her husband what God had done. He got saved because of that sign. She went to every dentist that had ever worked on her mouth to verify that they hadn't done that dental work. They all said that the gold in her mouth was too fine and they didn't use that quality of gold. This miracle took place in a town north of Oslo.

After that meeting I went outside for some fresh air. It was late in the evening and the midnight sun had just set. I saw spectacular colours in the sky moving to and fro. The locals who were with me were amazed and remarked that it was not the right time of the year for it to appear. For two nights the lights appeared every time we came out of our meetings.

At another time I was on the west coast of Norway where I had taught the young people to face north and to call to the aurora borealis to come to the light of their shining. I was teaching them a principle even if it wasn't the right season for the lights. Gold dust was manifesting in our meetings and as we looked out the window, the aurora borealis was pulsating in the sky. We were teaching our people how to be *ets chay*, the Tree of Life. We must give creation something to arc with: the crown of our heads, understanding, wisdom, knowledge, justice, judgment, grace and mercy, glory, splendour and awe, victory and endurance, divine creativity, and rest. The Northern Lights were responding to us and it was great!

This is why we teach the menorah and the Tree of Life because astonishing things happen. Recently I was at some meetings and somehow we jumped time and had so much more time available to us than anticipated. I also saw this happen with my British passport. I had applied for one and I was calling it in because I needed to get to America for a conference. On the 24th of that month I received a letter through the post telling me that my passport would arrive on the 25th which was the next day. A few hours later there was a knock on my door and my passport had arrived. I signed for it and saw that the document was dated for two days later. I received it before it was officially sent! I was able to catch my flight the next day which was the day I should have received my passport.

I've had passport stamps dated for twenty years in the future while everyone else in my group has that day's date stamped in theirs. This is an outworking of me reaching into the *olam*, my future. I open my spirit so I can emanate the light from within thereby pulling things inwards. We cannot let something out if it's not inside. We must practice honouring the points on the tree of life and practice calling things to the light of our shining and see what Yahweh will do with us.

Chapter 7
Praying In Tongues

I have heard it said that if you are two, then you're more than, but if you're one, you are less than. Community is vital, team is vital, co-labouring is vital. If there is one man doing one thing, he will be less than, but if we corporately arc together with a team within our community it brings about multiplication, bringing about something authentic, which can be revealed within honour on the face of the earth.

I feel there are people who have been engaging with some things and these teachings are helping them to sit on their mountain, engage with Yahweh's Mountain, engaging with the menorah and the *sefirot*. I believe that many things they have been praying for and trusting for will have a breakthrough and I feel the transformation in the answer to prayer that is coming to them will give them the capacity to sit within that place as a king, to govern, rule and reign over the breakthrough they will administrate. They will not say, "Yahweh, I'm praying for an answer to this prayer and waiting for You to bring the answer." I feel that what has unfolded for us will enable them to go in and administrate what it looks like and what needs to take place in order to administrate that breakthrough so it no longer becomes an answer to prayer, which is waiting to materialize, but it has already happened.

Every prayer that we pray, should manifest as the answer into the midst of creation. It's the reason that in Scripture we don't find Yeshua teaching us how to deal with unanswered prayer! We were not meant to live on the face of the earth with unanswered prayer. The unanswered prayers we see within the Church Age are because of the immaturity and the lack of responsibility we carry on the face of the earth. If we've traded into that we have a distorted view of our engagement with Yahweh, whether it be through prayer or requests made known.

Many Christians do not pray, they complain. We go into our prayer closet and complain to Yahweh about everything that is not right. That's not prayer. Something completely different is happening within the maturity of sons. Now, our prayer is not complaining, we're taking responsibility within the union, going in, to spend time to behold in the mountain those things that are happening within us, and the requests that we have are sitting within us as sons, and we now get to administrate that into creation, regardless of the prayer that we're praying and the answer that we're waiting for.

I believe so many people will get the answers to their prayers because of their position as sons, understanding the process to be there, and to administrate what is happening in the Kingdom Realms, seated in creation through them as a son.

I've had to untangle myself from a religious belief system masquerading as inferior truth on the topic of prayer, because the way it was modelled in the Church structure was not the truth according to how Yeshua modelled it and how we should be living within a lifestyle of prayer.

John 15:1-7, "I am the true vine, and My Father is the vinedresser. Every branch in Me that does not bear fruit, He takes away; and every branch that bears fruit He prunes it so that it may bear more fruit. You are already clean because of the word which I have spoken to you. Abide in Me, and I in you. As the branch cannot bear fruit of itself unless it abides in the vine, so neither can you unless you abide in Me. I am the vine, you are the branches; he who abides in Me and I in him, he bears much fruit, for apart from Me you can do nothing. If anyone does not abide in Me, he is thrown away as a branch and dries up; and they gather them, and cast them into the fire and they are burned. If you abide in Me, and My words abide in you, ask whatever you wish, and it will be done for you."

During our belief and our pursuit, a realm opens up and we begin to engage in truth and there are several times that Yeshua says, "I tell you the truth," before making a statement that gets everyone's attention and brings about a massive transformation to mindsets and beliefs because He deals at a level that is far greater than we can comprehend. In the aforementioned Scripture Yeshua says He is the true vine and His Father is the gardener and cuts off every branch in Yeshua that doesn't bear fruit. Many times we feel we're in a season where Yahweh is cutting off the branches. We're pursuing, walking, and engaging and then we realize there are things surfacing within us because of the process and our desire for maturity. Yahweh is saying to us that He loves us enough that He has to cut off those things that are bearing no fruit. The very things we thought were important to us and sitting within the structure of who we are, are connected to a system which bears no fruit. Because of our desire and pursuit Yahweh has to cut off those branches because they're not bearing fruit. The branches that we sometimes depend upon are the very branches that could keep us in a place of immaturity. Walking through this process in union with Yahweh and our desire for maturity, He has to cut it off as we're on a journey going from glory to glory. In my own life Yahweh has cut some things off that I thought meant something, meantime they meant absolutely nothing!

Yeshua then says He is going to prune the branches that do bear fruit because if He does this the branches will become more fruitful. If we're going through a pruning stage we mustn't confuse it with Yahweh disciplining us. He has so much in store for us and the very thing that is seated within us and bearing fruit must be pruned so it can bear more. This is the process of maturity and the more we understand our function as a son the more we walk in understanding that we're being transformed into the image of our Father and we are quick to understand that whatever needs to be pruned is so that what we carry within the next phase of the journey is going to allow us to have the responsibility to carry in the midst of creation. What we are engaging with on this journey is manifesting something within us.

Many times the confirmation of the fruit that is happening comes from people giving us affirmation and because of this validation from man we begin to think that we're bearing fruit because of the response, but within the Kingdom Yahweh wants to prune us because of what we are about to behold as a son. *We must not allow what man is saying to dictate to us the level of maturity in which we will walk.*

At times, the way we comprehend prayer under the sun and the religious process, is that we must find time to go into a quiet room, make sure to not be interrupted, setting the atmosphere with worship music, and then we release the prayer. When we finish we sit back to wait and to watch what will happen to the prayer that we prayed. Even mystics can easily fall into the trap of praying religiously. They might be using different terminology but the religious practice is the same. They might think they will change things spiritually to bring about a transformation in the natural. This will not work because prayer is about union with Yahweh. Yeshua would often shift Himself away from the crowd and Scripture says He would go up the mountain to pray. There might not have been physical mountains within the region He was ministering, so where did He go? He would shift into the Mountain of Yahweh and in that place, behold the union with His

Father. We have the same access to spend time in union with the Father through prayer and intimacy, to engage with Him and to take on the countenance of the very One we are engaging with. When Yeshua came out of the Mountain and was again present within the midst of creation, He would say, "I only do what I see my Father do. I only say what I hear My Father say." They were in union together, walking out the testimony scroll in the midst of creation. That is prayer. Christians have formulated a system of prayer which is in Church life today that is disjointed and disconnected and comes from insecurity because of not understanding their position, so selfish prayers are prayed.

John 15 says we must remain in Him so that our union will be of one heart and mind and assignment so when we walk out as a son in the midst of creation, what we begin to declare and frame and release is from His heart and echoes into creation because of our union. As I've untangled myself from so much, I have no recollection of how I used to pray because as I'm positioned as a son seated with my Father understanding what the union looks like. Within, my spirit man is deeply connected with Yahweh as He sits and governs over my spirit man. Yeshua sits and governs over my soul and *Ruach haKodesh* sits and rules and governs and has a co-labouring relationship over my body. So within the three-part being of who I am, I arc with the three-part being of who They are, (the three in one). Within the Three they have their function and within my three I have my function, (I'm three but I'm one) and within this union that takes place, I can engage securely knowing that I'm in Him and He's in me which has become a belief that is now so secure in the root of who I am that when I walk in creation and I speak, it's as if I'm praying.

Maybe there are still so many unanswered prayers from believers because within this process of their journey, Yahweh wants to invite them into a co-labouring relationship so that they understand their responsibility that they carry, and when they begin to speak and frame and declare things, they begin to see the answer manifest because of who they are as a son. Within the religious system that's one thing that speaks other than what the Kingdom Realm speaks about us. What happens within the Church Age? We say, "It's not about us, it's all God." We've adopted a false mindset which shuts gates in our ability to behold truth inside of us and we delay the answers that sit within the core of who we are.

One evening I was engaging in prayer and asking so many questions because I had realized how much I had traded into which was keeping me in bondage and I realized I needed to untangle from so much, but I was willing to do it, regardless of the cost. As I was talking to Yahweh about prayer I had a sense that the prayer we've adopted as the Church is not the truth and I knew there needed to be a different gateway but didn't know how to transition. I was spending time thinking and pondering on this. One morning I woke up early, spending time in my religious prayer, speaking out my unanswered prayers that I wanted to see come into my reality. As I was praying I felt myself leave my body and I (my natural man) was on the outside, looking at my body which I now know is my carnal man. My natural man was watching my carnal man pray religiously because it was rooted in religion and I was asking myself what I was doing! *My carnal man stopped praying and my natural man began to engage my spirit man in its rightful position and then it started to unfold.* It's not about the religious practice of praying, it's about union, aligning and arcing the different spiritual bodies to begin to engage in this union that **John 15** speaks about. As I'm in Him and He is in me, Scripture says we may ask anything we want and it will be given because of the responsibility and the mandate upon our life.

Within this relationship and what is unfolding for my wife and

I, because of our pursuit and our engagement and marriage of fifteen years, we know each other's desires. We were attending an online conference and the trading floor opened up. As this was unfolding, she touched my hand and her desire became my desire while my desire became her desire and through union, without having to say a word, we knew together what we needed to trade.

In my engagement with Yahweh, my desires become His and His become mine and without saying a word. When I am seated in creation and I frame what I'm feeling as if Yahweh's framing it, there is no religious practice but a union. When I speak, it's materializing, I'm creating and framing. If my Father created me in His image is it not true that I too can create because my Father is a creator? It's not just by the words I say but through desire and through thought and these begin to arc and align together and I see things start to manifest because of the desire of my heart.

When I teach, I can see gates open up and those who have gone before us who are in the Kingdom Realms pop in and ask me to speak about something that they have journeyed together with me. As I share it they can arc together with you so that it can become a possibility for you. When we read about Moshe in Scripture we can often marvel about the things that we think God did for him, like the time he parted the Red Sea so the people could walk on dry land and we wish Yahweh could do that for us. Yahweh didn't do that for Moshe. Moshe did it because of the union that he had with Yahweh. There's a big difference. He carried the authority and government when he was seated within the Kingdom Realms, arcing together with who he was. Scripture says he lifted his staff and the waters parted. He did it because of his union with Yahweh. We have the capacity to shift things in the midst of creation because we're learning the function and mandate we carry as a son. We are not inferior. There is no void between us and Yahweh and all that is within the Kingdom. We begin to fashion, form, and create the impossible because of our union with the Father and His union with us, in creation.

In **2 Corinthians 3:7-10** we read, "But if the ministry of death, written and engraved on stones, was glorious, so that the children of Israel could not look steadily at the face of Moses because of the glory of his countenance, which glory was passing away, how will the ministry of the Spirit not be more glorious? For if the ministry of condemnation had glory, the ministry of righteousness exceeds much more in glory. For even what was made glorious had no glory in this respect, because of the glory that excels."

Within the process I've gone through, I've spoken about the different Kingdoms. When I went to the Heaven of Heavens and was engaging with some things, Moshe appeared through a gateway, stood before me and the honour and gratitude that he showed towards me as a son, blew me away. When I read about him in Scripture, I'm the one who is impressed! As he engaged with me, his staff arced with my staff and this Scripture began to resonate within me and he was saying that sons are starting to step into the fullness of who they are and its unfolding for them is going to make his glory seem as if it was no glory at all.

Our mindsets need to be adjusted! In 2 **Corinthians 3:11-18** we read, "For if what is passing away was glorious, what remains is much more glorious. Therefore, since we have such hope, we use great boldness of speech — unlike Moses, who put a veil over his face so that the children of Israel could not look steadily at the end of what was passing away. But their minds were blinded. For until this day the same veil remains unlifted in the reading of the Old Testament, because the veil is taken away in Christ. But even to this day, when Moses is read, a veil lies on their heart. Nevertheless when one turns to the Lord, the veil is taken away. Now the Lord is the Spirit; and where the Spirit of the Lord is, there is liberty. But we all, with unveiled face, beholding as in a mirror the glory of the Lord, are being transformed into the same image from glory to glory, just as by the Spirit of the Lord."

Paul showed me that the veil which he mentioned in this Scripture is the veil of religion. The very veil that prevents Christians from stepping out of the Kingdom of the Earth still sits over their minds. This veil is not taken away by the sinner's prayer but by turning to Yahweh. This all comes through our union and relationship with Him and our engagement and pursuit, going in and arcing, beholding the mystery and supply of the secrets of Yahweh so we can begin to see it cultivated within us so we can fashion, form, and release it into creation.

Prayer is deeply connected to praying by the Spirit which is praying in tongues and has been lacking within us as sons and mystics. Within our tribe, because of various other interests and flavours of the moment that people have focused on, it has taken away the truth and importance and power of praying by the Spirit. If we can stay focused on praying in the Spirt for one hour, totally engrossed and engaged in the moment, we will start to see things happen which have never been seen on the face of the earth. When we pray in the Spirit it shifts so much of what is happening spiritually bringing massive break-through. I see so many people engaging with other things that have taken its place, honouring those things, rather than the very thing that brings about massive break-through which is speaking in tongues.

What fell upon the people of The Way in the Book of Acts? *Ruach haKodesh* fell on them and then started to burn on the inside of them. They began praying in the Spirit which brought about great transformation and yet two-thousand years later, because of the religious spirit that people have traded into, it has tried to silence the very thing that brings about transformation.

Within my engagement and understanding the union of my Father, sitting within that place and praying in the Spirit, I love to engage in the Realm of Mystery. It's this realm that brought about such transformation in my own life. I sit and engage within that realm and I honour it. Recently I arced with a conference that happened a few years ago in the United Kingdom, where Grant Mahoney was teaching about the secrets. I had no framework for what 'secrets' meant within the Kingdom coming from the heart of Yahweh. By faith I started to engage so that it could become part of who I am. Recently Ian Clayton was teaching about the difference between the secrets of Yahweh and the mysteries of Yahweh. A desire opened in me that I've never seen before and it came because I honour the mystery. A gate opened into another realm, to begin to behold the secrets of Yahweh which are different to the mysteries of Yahweh. His mysteries are kept under the sun but the secrets are found above the sun. In **Proverbs 25:2** we read, "It is the glory of God to conceal a matter, but the glory of kings is to search out a matter."

This leads us to **John 3** where Nicodemus has a conversation with Yeshua who explains to Nicodemus how someone is born again. He asks Yeshua how he's supposed to go back into his mother's womb and Yeshua asked how he didn't know this if he was a rabbi. If Nicodemus couldn't understand what Yeshua was saying, how was he going to have a framework to see that which has no earthly parallel? Yeshua was speaking to Nicodemus from a Realm of Mystery, building a framework for him to understand so that the Realm of Mystery positioned under the sun would be able to arc together to manifest something in creation. It's in the Realm of Mystery that we can honour and walk it out so that it becomes a gateway for us to behold the secrets of Yahweh which have no earthly parallel. Within the mysteries, Yeshua was still speaking to Nicodemus giving him an earthly platform to begin to establish how one is born again. What was happening in the natural was arcing with the spiritual in the mysteries, but still under the sun. Yahweh was extending an invitation to Nicodemus that would allow him to behold the secrets that have no earthly parallel.

This has been entrusted to us as sons. Not just the mysteries but the secrets. We are about to bring about such a redemption upon the face of the earth, because of our honour and our journey together and our maturity. This is opening up gates for us to be seated and fully enveloped by the secrets that are forming so that when we walk in creation we are establishing His Kingdom on the earth. **Matthew 6:10**, "Your kingdom come. Your will be done on earth as it is in heaven."

ACTIVATION

I want you to engage and set your heart in motion for what is unfolding for you. Pray in the Spirit as I administrate some things. By faith start to engage with what is unfolding in your mountain within you as a son. Engagement is not about ascension but about being seated together in that place. I want you to be fully aware of what is unfolding for you.

Yahweh, as we begin to engage, we engage with the unfolding supply of what is happening within us as sons within the engagement, within the union and understanding the importance of a lifestyle of prayer, not religiously but through the union that we have with You. We begin to behold what is unfolding within us and we engage as we begin to go into the places within your mountain, to begin to behold what is unfolding, the transformation that is our portion right now.

We honour you, Faith, for who you are. We honour you, Hope, for who you are and we thank you for the desire to engage. For faith

110

is the substance of things hoped for, it is the evidence of things not yet seen and we step into this right now. Begin to feel what is unfolding within your temple, your body, as you are an arc. Allow it to pulsate through the gates of who you are to begin to establish what is happening.

Chapter 8
Praying In The Spirit

Yahweh has been speaking to me on the subject of praying in tongues. We have come to a place where we feel that tongues is antiquated and from an old age, but tongues is not that. It is vitally important and we have substituted it by saying the *Yod Hey Vav Hey*, speaking in Hebrew or meditating and we stopped engaging in tongues. I felt Yahweh impress on me to gather as a group and press into speaking in tongues. The first time we got together, we managed to go for fifteen minutes before some started to revert to *Yod, Hey, Vav, Hey* and speaking in their home language. We had to make the effort to only speak in tongues. It was quite hard because we had to start engaging in tongues in a different way and a different place so we could do this effectively.

There are different types of tongues, and they are really important. This isn't a gift that we only get when we engage with Yahweh because people can lay hands on us for us to receive the ability. It's vital that we speak in tongues, especially in the day and the age we are living in now, because of what it does – it edifies us and builds us up in our most holy faith – it releases something on the inside of us. It also starts to release something on the face of the earth. I began to see a trend around the world of people calling for times to be set aside for speaking in tongues in mainline Churches, charismatic Churches, Pentecostal Churches, and the prophetic movement. I know some ministers who say that most of their prayer is done in tongues.

Recently I heard a prophet say we have become averse to the secrets and mysteries of Yahweh. The Church doesn't want to go into the "weird stuff"! This pertains primarily to Europe because of secular humanism and not wanting to offend people. My husband and I planted a Church in Victoria Falls, Zimbabwe, and one of the Tour Guides said to me that we would get far more people coming to Church if we didn't speak in tongues, because it offended them. The most influential couple in the city came to one of our meetings. During the service they made a commotion, picked up their things and left. They sent a message saying that if we wanted to know what was wrong we needed to see them. We weren't that interested but we did see them and they told us they didn't want us to speak in tongues because it was offensive. They wanted a Church in town that would be nice to people and make them feel good for the week ahead. I drew a line on the table with my finger and told him that I had just drawn a line in the sand and he shouldn't cross it and that we would speak in tongues in that Church whether he liked it or not. Another group came and said that if worship were shorter and not so loud, more people would come to the Church. My husband thanked them for their input and the following week he added twenty minutes on to the already one-hour long worship. People were so under the influence of *Ruach haKodesh* that we had to carry them out. Needless to say, they also left. So we see that a mystery averseness has come in where people don't want the mysteries or the strange.

Grant Mahoney shared that he believes that before Yahweh created the living letters His communication was done through a 'heavenly language' which we would call 'tongues.'

They did not speak in Hebrew. Yahweh created the living letters so that He could say, "Let there be light." The letter could then engage and make the light in the creation process.

Speaking in tongues is speaking in the language of angels and the language of Yahweh. It is a strange tongue, as in babbling of lips, and is not understood here on earth. There is also the speaking in the tongues of men which are known languages. If you are a mystic, you must be baptized in the Holy Spirit! As a teen I had heard about being baptized in the Holy Spirit but was too shy to ask anyone to pray for me. I heard someone say that I should ask Yahweh to baptize me and then say whatever came to mind. Tongues cannot be said in your head, it has to come out of your mouth. I knelt next to my bed and asked Yeshua to baptize me. I tried to say what was in my head but I felt it wasn't working, and feeling idiotic, I went to bed. The second night was the same and I just made guttural noises. My granny was a very devout Christian who loved Yeshua and she would kneel next to her bed to read the Word and pray, so that was my model. On the third night, while I was kneeling next to my bed making guttural sounds, all of a sudden out of my mouth flew my 'tongue' and it was fluent. My husband's experience was different and he only got a few words initially. The more he prayed, the more his 'tongue' grew and more words would come. This was how I got baptized in the Holy Spirit with the evidence of speaking in tongues.

There are many doctrines which say it isn't necessary to speak in tongues to be baptized in the Holy Spirit. When we are baptized in the Holy Spirit, the power comes from on high to imbue us with power and the evidence does seem to show tongues. Tongues was restored to the Age of the *ecclesia* in 1906 through the Azusa Street revival. This was also a prevalent doctrine in the 1980s which we began to throw away as we became mystery averse but honestly, there is usually a manifestation of tongues that comes from a person once they've been baptized in the Holy Spirit.

In **1 Corinthians 14:2** we read, "For he who speaks in a tongue does not speak to men but to God, for no one understands him; however, in the spirit he speaks mysteries."

The word 'mystery' is *mysterion* in Greek and is a neuter noun. It is mentioned over twenty-eight times in the New Testament and means partnering with the hidden thing or secrets or mysteries, which should be normal for us. We know there are the secrets of Yahweh and the mysteries of Yahweh. Mystery is two things; secrets and mysteries, so when we speak, it's a hidden or a secret thing and not obvious to the understanding, a hidden purpose or counsels, secrets of God, secret counsels with which God governs the righteous.

The following Scriptures mention these mysteries:

Matthew 13:10-11, "And the disciples came and said to Him, 'Why do You speak to them in parables?' He answered and said to them, 'Because it has been given to you to know the mysteries of the kingdom of heaven, but to them it has not been given.'"

Mark 4:10-11, "But when He was alone, those around Him with the twelve asked Him about the parable. And He said to them, 'To you it has been given to know the mystery of the kingdom of God; but to those who are outside, all things come in parables.'"

Luke 8:10, "And He said, 'To you it has been given to know the mysteries of the kingdom of God, but to the rest it is given in parables.'"

Romans 11:25a, "For I do not desire, brethren, that you should be ignorant of this mystery."

1 Corinthians 4:1, "Let a man so consider us, as servants of Christ and stewards of the mysteries of God."

Recently I heard someone say we don't need the mysteries and that there are no more secrets with God but honestly, there are no more mysteries because they've all been found. Mysteries you seek out, you look for them, but secrets can only come with a face-to-face encounter with Yahweh. These might not be found in books!

Religion likes control and order more than it likes mysteries, sovereignty, and the secrets of Yahweh. We are entrusted with the mystical, the strange, the trances, the translocations, extreme tongues, and these are just scratching the surface of being a peculiar people. If you want the strange and the *mysterion* in your life you can't have them on your own terms. My husband and I were married for twenty-three years. We had some odd things happen in our ministry over the years which are on-going. I reminded Ricky how we used to have a prayer meeting before church where we prayed and sang in tongues for an hour and then we would have the crazy stuff happen with angels arriving at our meetings. I remember Ricky playing guitar when his angel appeared in front of him and there were multi-coloured feathers floating around his feet. He fell face forward over the monitor and the mic stand onto his guitar. We had such unusual things happening apart from gold teeth, feathers, oil, and rain inside the building. These all came from a place of speaking in tongues and not being mystery averse, but being open to signs.

Signs are there to point you to something to make you wonder at the wonder and awe and splendour and beauty of Yahweh. We are so immature, that when the signs and wonders happen we chase the signs and wonders and the one through whom they come. We idolize the five-fold ministries and idolize those through whom the signs and wonders happen. We must be careful that we don't chase after the 'stuff' because it's a lesser form of glory than that which is found in heaven. The gold that we see here is a lesser form of the glory and gold that is in heaven. I'd rather be like Solomon who constituted gold so plenteously that it lay in the streets like stones than having tiny specks falling in a meeting.

I like both! We would have nuggets falling in our meetings and would take cello tape to pick up the gold and silver that had fallen and chase after these things, looking for gold teeth. It got to a point that if we didn't have precious stones manifest in the meeting, then it wasn't a meeting at all and it lifted off us. We didn't know how to administer the glory and that which was an outworking of the glory and having precious stones fall in the meeting doesn't necessarily mean God was in the meetings but it was an outworking of the worship we gave Him. He loves us and just wants to pour it out.

We don't often get what we want because this is not about us. If someone died today, in this studio, and were raised from the dead on live stream, there would be a long queue outside the door tomorrow, for healing, especially in these days with COVID-19. People chase after giftings and not after the Giver of this gifting. We must become part of the signs and wonders. During the 1980s and 1990s the signs and wonders came through understanding faith and speaking in tongues. At the time we didn't understand that Faith was a Being, we thought it was a force but we honoured Faith and turned towards it so Faith honoured us and turned towards us. As a result there were massive signs and wonders and we must get back there. I understand there are ebbs and flows and Yahweh takes away and restores things but we're not seeing many people being healed. There is a revival of worship and intimacy with Yahweh at the moment because He is untangling us from the idolizing of the five-fold ministry and idolizing those through whom this comes.

There *are* those who carry the mysteries on the face of the earth, like Ian Clayton. Grant Mahoney has the most intense ability to see the angelic, to know their name and their function in our lives. Marios Ellinas has the most intense ability to teach about honour and finances. They are Rabbis to us and teach us the mysteries, however they never want to be in a position where they are idolized and where we call them Pastor, Prophet, Evangelist, Teacher or Apostle. These are functions, not titles!

Signs and wonders must be around us and we must become part of them. A few weeks ago we were in Cape Town, South Africa. I had hurt my Achilles tendon and was in so much pain I could hardly walk. I was supposed to go up Table Mountain the following day to redeem some things because of a fire they had had. We were in a meeting that evening and I didn't want to make a big deal of it, so just sat still. Ricky began to speak and was sharing about a time that he had hurt his knee and he was asking Yahweh to heal him because he's a long-distance runner and his knee hurt too much for him to be able to run. It was almost as if Yahweh rebuked him and said, "I can't heal it because you don't love your body and you don't love your knee." So he went somewhere private and started loving on his knee and talking to it and began to restore it verbally. Yahweh healed his knee!

While I was sitting in that meeting, I was listening but not expecting to get healed, and Ricky said, "Imagine if that which is in me now, the healing virtue that came on me because I honoured my knee and loved on my knee, opened up and came out of me and touched everyone that is around me." We spoke about the *sefirot*, the Tree of Life in us that comes out of us. I was sitting on my chair thinking about how Peter came out of his prayer closet and went to the synagogue and everyone called for the sick and needy because they knew his shadow would touch them. The overshadowing of the glory he was sitting in because he'd probably gone into the Pool of Everything, seeing how healing came in its original form, had taken it on the inside of him and when he walked out, everywhere he went his overshadowing healed everyone.

During this whole process I felt nothing, and at the end of the meeting I stood up to talk to some of the youngsters and I realized my heel was fine. I decided not to say anything in case it got sore later. After the meeting I walked to the car normally and the next day I was able to walk up Table Mountain. The folks with me had seen how I struggled to get on the plane the day before and I reminded them about what Ricky had said. Imagine if what was in us came out of us and that place where we had been in the secrets of Yahweh and began to assimilate the beauty and healing of Yahweh on our bodies and in us, so much so that when we opened up our spirits the fragrance of Christ would come out of us to a dying world and they would get healed by the frequency of what was overshadowing us. When Rick said that my head went off into another space and I was completely healed.

This is new school but actually ancient school. We've forgotten how to love and to be the mysteries. The aforementioned prophet was saying that there will be known tongues as in a known language and unknown tongues which are in the secrets and mysteries which will be huge tools for evangelism. I was speaking in tongues a while ago and someone told me I was speaking in Hebrew. Another time I was speaking in tongues in front of someone and he asked me what language I was speaking. I did this on purpose and told him I speak a few languages but this was a heavenly language. He just stared at me and said he thought I was speaking in French.

We've made the application of tongues too small and God is downloading the mysteriousness of speaking in tongues into the people so that the unknown and the known tongue will be in us. We must speak heaven's language of mysteries and earth's language of known tongues. Earth's language is when we speak in tongues and release finances, art, business and so forth and heaven's language is the mysteries and secrets of Yahweh that begin to come and fall on us. This prophet said we will see this in a moment but as quickly as the moment comes it will be gone. We must not lose that place where He's opening that window to speak in tongues which accesses the secrets and the mysteries of Yahweh.

Once I was praying and arcing with my spirit man and seeing it worship in great abandonment before Yahweh, speaking in tongues. I was arcing in tongues in the spirit and in the flesh, learning how to see myself do that. This prophet mentioned that we will come into that place of ecstatic tongues, worship, and prophecy and it will be a moment in time where Yahweh will release it and we need to hold on to it. Speaking in tongues is not old technology but is both a modern and an ancient technology. If we say we don't need to speak in tongues anymore it means we know all the mysteries and have all the secrets of Yahweh.

I have to build myself up in my most holy faith learning to manifest it through the *yesod* of divine creativity and through the *tifferet* where living waters flow out of my belly so I can release it through the *malkuth* where my feet touch the earth. In **Romans 8:19** we read that the whole of creation is groaning, waiting for the manifestation of sons, for me to build myself up in order to release it into creation. The prophet carried on and said that when we speak in tongues we calibrate our cells to become integrated into the mysteries. There are so many studies that show what happens in the brain and the body when we speak in tongues. Scripture says that when we speak in tongues we do not speak to people but to God by speaking in mysteries. Speaking in tongues begins to affect our DNA in the Tree of Life so that it starts to recalibrate our body for us to be a receiver of mysteries and a bringer of mysteries and like a magnet begin to draw and attract mysteries into our life.

The *Ruach ha Kodesh* will then say it's time for Him to release the mysteries which we have downloaded into our DNA, through building ourselves up in our most holy faith, which can then go out into the earth. This is because we speak in mysteries and begin to understand it because we integrate ourselves into the mysteries and into the deep *sod* (secret or confidential conversation) of Elohim. As we begin to do this and it permeates through us we can begin to open up our spirit and what's in us comes out of us. In **Acts 3:6** we read, "Then Peter said, 'Silver and gold I do not have, but what I do have I give you: In the name of Jesus Christ of Nazareth, rise up and walk.'" In the name of *Yod Hey Vav Hey*, breathing Him in and out in that place of Yahweh, the secrets of Yahweh, rise up and walk.

Being *in the Name* does not mean we just say it as part of a prayer and use it like a magic wand. It's breathing in the Name of Yahweh and placing myself in the Name so I can then say like in **Acts 17:28a**, "In Him we live and move and have our being."

Colossians 1:27 says, "To them God willed to make known what are the riches of the glory of this mystery among the Gentiles: which is Christ in you, the hope of glory."

When Scripture says that whatever we ask in His Name we will receive, the word 'in' means inside, so I can go into His name and I stand there and breathe Him in and then breathe out through my body, through my belly, down through my feet, by pulling from the Realms of the Kingdom into my body and then pulling the mysteries down through my feet because every place our feet shall tread, Yahweh has given it to us and released the mysteries and the secrets.

Speaking in tongues integrates us into divinity and into the divine. It transmutes our desire into what *Ruach haKodesh* is saying and then we can truly pray. We do have to turn our attention into *Ruach haKodesh* and look at Him to see what He is doing because we don't know how to pray but He prays on our behalf. We can get distracted when speaking in tongues. We can watch TV, be nervous, read a book and pick up the trash. When I practice and train my flesh to stop it and to behave, I close my ears and speak in tongues because then that's all I hear and I concentrate on the words coming out of my mouth even though I don't understand them because it's a heavenly language but my spirit understands. This is a great way to practice turning our intent and desire towards *Ruach haKodesh* so that when I speak in tongues I transmute my desire into Him and what He is saying and I then truly begin to pray.

We were assistant Pastors in a church with an auditorium that could seat 1500 people and the Church consisted of about 1100 people. We were having a massive revival through worship and all sorts of crazy things were happening. We lost about one hundred people because our worship was wild and about five hundred joined us. The Satanists and witchdoctors were coming against us and the harder they pushed, the harder we pushed. An American band called The Resurrection Band were coming to the Church for a concert. They were a Christian heavy metal group that had a huge impact in impoverished and underprivileged communities in their local town. One of the people in Church told us that a group of local Satanists, called the Coffin Kids, were coming to the concert. Many people were in an uproar when they found out and we thought how would they hear the gospel if they don't come to church?

Prior to this concert we had spent a few weeks praying in tongues after work and on weekends. Just before the concert it was our area's turn, about forty of us, to be on prayer duty and, in the spirit, turned our intent towards Yahweh and began to intercede, worship, and pray in tongues. That's all we did until our tongues turned into groaning like we were in labour and that night I gave birth in the spirit two or three times to something. We left the prayer room at about 02:30 a.m. to go down to the auditorium where my husband said we were to walk around in silence seven times and then give a shout to the Lord because the Bible says that the shout of a king is in the midst of his people. We walked around that place in silence and after the seventh time, on the count of three, we shouted to the Lord. Something sucked up our shout, like a sweet-smelling sacrifice, and our loud shout just disappeared. Yahweh had leaned over and had inhaled our shout.

This happened around 03:00 a.m. and after that we went home. At that moment, the senior Pastor woke up and phoned us to ask what just happened because Yahweh had told him that a major citadel had fallen in the city that night. This happened because of speaking in tongues. This major citadel was a stronghold of religion that had fallen that night and when the young Satanists came to hear Resurrection Band play, many of them got saved and left their craft all because a major citadel had fallen. This happened all because we had turned our intent to Yahweh, and because we had prayed in tongues and in the spirit with groanings that could not be uttered, and Father did something spectacular and supernatural.

Tongues is a living gateway into the realms of the mysteries and the secrets of Yahweh. Mysteries can be sought out while secrets come to those who are in true relationship with Yahweh. You will not find secrets in a book and if some are, they are so hidden that they're not visible any longer. I was in an amazing place of deep worship to Yahweh, engaging with two Beings and they gave me a name that I could address Yahweh with. I called a Jewish friend to ask her what this meant because I had never heard it before. She asked me who had given me that name because the Jews have hidden it and it's not a name that is used or mentioned because it's a closely guarded secret. Only Adam used that name in the garden when he walked with Yahweh. I can't reveal that name because it's a closely guarded secret only given to friends. This secret was given to me from a place of intimacy with Yahweh.

David said in **Psalm 51:11**, "Do not cast me away from Your presence, and do not take Your Holy Spirit from me." There were things that David did and places he accessed because he spoke in tongues and had the *Ruach haKodesh* with him. Tongues take the language of the Spirit and turn it into matter. Through quantum physics we take the waves of frequency and turn our attention to it so by looking at it, transmute it into matter. Tongues does the same thing by creating a bridge or doorway into the secrets of Yahweh. The spirit-man gets strong and begins to truly reign over your triune being. The body, soul, and spirit start to come into unity and into divine sovereignty when we speak in tongues.

To say that tongues is defunct has been a reason for us to lose the signs, wonders, and miracles and Yahweh wants to restore it back to us, to the Church, and into your life today. All over the world people are praying in tongues, framing the mysteries and secrets over our cities, counties, provinces, states, and countries. Your speaking in tongues is also creating a gateway or pathway within you for the secrets and the mysteries of Yahweh. This is a short season where we don't have a lot of time to step through and take hold of what it has for us by once more releasing signs, wonders, and miracles. This might not be the same as what we saw before with healing on the streets, it could be something completely different now. Perhaps whatever overshadows me will overshadow those who are around me and healing happens and business will take place and things will come to the light of my shining and people's lives will be touched just because you or I are in a room. As a Church, we hired a school venue and the Principal asked us not to leave because things had changed dramatically for the school. Finances had come to them, children were being enrolled and the blessing stayed on them because of the frequency that sits on us as we operate as sons in the Realms of the Kingdom. We need to strengthen our triune beings especially in the days we are living in and we need to get back into the habit of speaking in tongues in our spirit, in our flesh, in the natural and the physical and the spiritual. We must get together with a group and start speaking in tongues without being religious about it but rather turning our intent with purpose towards *Ruach haKodesh* and when we do that He transmutes our desire into His and then we are truly praying.

I cannot tell you the amount of signs and wonders we've seen as a result of speaking in tongues. If it's good enough for Yahweh, it's good enough for me! Speaking in tongues when the demons are manifesting, speaking in tongues when the aliens are manifesting, speaking in tongues when people need healing, we've seen signs and wonders follow that mysterion, the mystery that we speak as we speak in tongues and the ruach starts to flow over people. When I speak in tongues I do not speak to people but to God because no one understands, but in the spirit we speak mysterion, secrets and mysteries. All my children got baptized in the Holy Spirit and spoke in tongues when they were young, and no one prayed for them.

ACTIVATION

As an activation, we will now find a quiet place and speak in tongues so that we can release something inside of us and build ourselves up in our most holy faith so that it can flow from our belly through our feet into the *malkuth* and into the earth. In that place the earth can turn itself back into us and look at us as sons manifesting, and we will start to flow in the fullness of this as well.

While you pray in tongues you can put your hands on your belly and concentrate on the words coming out of your mouth, take hold of your thoughts and push through as this is growing your spirit and making it strong. As you pray you are bringing your body and soul into triune alignment. Begin to feel the secrets and the mysteries of Yahweh come as you lift up your head o you gate, coming down into your belly. See the Tree of Life on the inside of you and the menorah and your DNA being recalibrated by tongues. Let this language of the Spirit begin to come into matter and turning into something tangible within you. Now begin to release it through your body, through your feet and into the earth so that it responds to you. Breathe in and call out *Yod Hey Vav Hey* and breathe out. Breathe in, *Yod Hey Vav Hey*, and out.

In the realms of the Kingdom, wherever your body is ailing you I want you to take it before the throne and ask Yahweh to forgive you where you have dishonoured that part of your body.

Pray this, "I forgive myself for dishonouring my body and that part of my body. I honour my cellular structure, I honour my bones and my muscles. I honour my body and bring life to it because of the blood of the Lamb. In this place of honouring my body, I thank you Yahweh that whatever is in me can now come out of me. Silver and gold I do not have, but what I have I stand in Your Name, *Yod Hey Vav Hey*, rise up and walk. Thank You for healing."

This is how I want you to speak in tongues, keep your attention and your focus, downloading and building your spirit and releasing it into the earth and then repeating the process. In this way you will become a conduit for the goodness and the mercy and the glory of Yahweh and of His splendour and awe.

About Lindi

Lindi Masters has been in active ministry for 41 years. Her heart is to mentor the Body of Yeshua into 'Maturity being their Vav', rooted and grounded in YHVH and in His mysteries and secrets. Lindi has a legacy of 3 incredible children who have all married Godly partners and she has 4 beautiful grandchildren.

She currently divides her time between the UK and South Africa.

About Ricky

Ricky's heart is to challenge and encourage others on how to become Sons of Yahweh. He shares from his Kingdom encounters that have taught him about the importance of being positioned correctly as a Son, how to govern as a Son, journeying with Faith and untangling from the religious spirit.
Ricky is married to Melanie and together they have two children and reside in Durban, South Africa.

Made in United States
North Haven, CT
07 August 2023

40042629R00076